ROUTLEDGE LIBRARY EDITIONS:
AGING

I0095478

Volume 16

THE GENERATION
JIGSAW

THE GENERATION
JIGSAW

IRENE GORE

R Routledge
Taylor & Francis Group

LONDON AND NEW YORK

First published in 1976 by George Allen & Unwin Ltd

This edition first published in 2024
by Routledge
4 Park Square, Milton Park, Abingdon, Oxon OX14 4RN

and by Routledge
605 Third Avenue, New York, NY 10158

Routledge is an imprint of the Taylor & Francis Group, an informa business

© 1976 George Allen & Unwin (Publishers) Ltd

All rights reserved. No part of this book may be reprinted or reproduced or utilised in any form or by any electronic, mechanical, or other means, now known or hereafter invented, including photocopying and recording, or in any information storage or retrieval system, without permission in writing from the publishers.

Trademark notice: Product or corporate names may be trademarks or registered trademarks, and are used only for identification and explanation without intent to infringe.

British Library Cataloguing in Publication Data
A catalogue record for this book is available from the British Library

ISBN: 978-1-032-67433-9 (Set)
ISBN:978-1-032-69614-0 (Volume 16) (hbk)
ISBN: 978-1-032-69625-6 (Volume 16) (pbk)
ISBN: 978-1-032-69624-9 (Volume 16) (ebk)

DOI: 10.4324/9781032696249

Publisher's Note
The publisher has gone to great lengths to ensure the quality of this reprint but points out that some imperfections in the original copies may be apparent.

Disclaimer
The publisher has made every effort to trace copyright holders and would welcome correspondence from those they have been unable to trace.

THE GENERATION JIGSAW

Irene Gore

London   George Allen & Unwin Ltd
Ruskin House   Museum Street

First published in 1976

This book is copyright under the Berne Convention. All rights
are reserved. Apart from any fair dealing for the purpose of
private study, research, criticism or review, as permitted under
the Copyright Act, 1956, no part of this publication may be
reproduced, stored in a retrieval system, or transmitted, in any
form or by any means, electronic, electrical, chemical, mechanical,
optical, photocopying, recording or otherwise, without the prior
permission of the copyright owner. Enquiries should be addressed
to the publishers.

© George Allen & Unwin (Publishers) Ltd 1976

ISBN 0 04 613030 6 hardback
      0 04 613031 4 paperback

Printed in Great Britain
in 11 point Fournier type
by Cox & Wyman Ltd, London, Fakenham and Reading

To a charmer –
Catherine Matthews
of the limpid mind

Contents

Introduction

This book deals with relationships between younger and older people. Its purpose is not to generate problems where perhaps there are none, but to take a look at situations where they do exist. Its main concern is with the quality of life of older people.

In writing about human problems one inevitably has to generalise, and at the same time one realises that one's argument may not apply strictly to any particular individual. My hope remains, however, that from these generalisations some points will apply to some people, other points to others, and that something illuminating or helpful may emerge.

The more complex and specific problems faced by severely disadvantaged people – the invalids, the recluses, the destitute, the utterly neglected – lie outside the scope of this book. It is my conviction that the problems of the reasonably fit, reasonably independent majority of older people deserve to be considered. Therefore the discussion here is centred on situations involving such people and their juniors.

Life is a continuum, and getting older is simply continuing to be alive. People's abilities and qualities do not suddenly change or vanish. Most older people are far more capable and robust, in body and in spirit, than we tend to give them credit for. Their real need is for expansion. As T. S. Eliot has so perceptively said, 'old men ought to be explorers'. This view is at variance with many of our traditional attitudes which are reflected in our relationships with older people. These attitudes need to be revised because they create more problems than they solve.

The injunction to honour one's father and mother is part of our ethic, and we traditionally interpret this as 'taking care' of them. But 'taking care' of older people carries the risk of making them too passive, and dependent, of blurring their individuality. Their real well-being would be better served by treating them as people in their own right, and not as pets.

In our society, in general terms, the attitude to retirement is such that once people are no longer working their intrinsic worth is diminished. Yet people are retired compulsorily on grounds of age. In former times a person had something to look forward to in later years: the status which his experience gave him. Older people enjoyed the regard of the family and of the community. The tendency now is to channel and guide our elders into a mode of life which someone else considers is best for them. We encourage our children to strive for maturity and independence, but we do not tell them that their ultimate 'reward' is to be regarded and treated as children again.

My hope is that this book will bring into focus some views which are likely to lead to a livelier, more fulfilled community of people of all ages.

I am most grateful to a key person in my extended family, my husband Dr P. H. Gore, who has so constructively and patiently helped me with the final editing of the text.

London
January 1976

PART I

A Positive and Hopeful View of Ageing

1
Mental and Physical Decline Is Not Inevitable

Forget your birthdays and keep your enthusiasms

To achieve a positive and life-enhancing attitude towards our own 'old age' and to that of others, we need to have a positive base from which to start. I put 'old age' in inverted commas because I do not really know when old age begins or how it manifests itself: each one of us is different. There are people old in calendar terms who are fit and alert, and there are 'youngsters' in their teens who are inert, bored and mentally flabby. This fact, which we can all observe, gives us a vital clue: *calendar age itself is irrelevant to what we are or to what we do.* Calendar age does unfortunately matter, however, in situations such as compulsory retirement.

Our obsession with calendar age serves no useful purpose whatever. It is a divisive, destructive and dispiriting habit, and we should do all we can to stop thinking of age first and of the person second. People who judge what others do by their age, rather than by their abilities, character or fitness, presumably never stop to think what a phrase like 'at her age' is really supposed to mean. If a woman of fifty has the figure to wear trousers she will look far more suitably dressed wearing them than a girl of twenty wearing trousers whose hip measurements happen to be six inches larger. If a fit and lively person aged eighty wants to go exploring then he should go ahead and do it. A playwright friend very aptly says that people who prejudge others by their age are like carriers of disease. They do not show the signs of the illness themselves, but they infect with gloom those who come into contact with them. There are many people who have a natural ability to dismiss age from their thoughts, and simply to live. They are immensely fortunate and they are the ones from whom we should take inspiration and courage. Animals, too, can serve us as examples. They know nothing of their own age, and if they are healthy they behave in a natural and lively way. A fifteen-year-old cat can frisk about like a kitten because it is unfettered by any notions of what is 'suitable' for its age. Phrases like 'Oh, I am too old for this' or 'It is too late for me to start on that' are often euphemisms used for 'Oh, I am not interested in this' or 'I cannot be bothered with that'.

My plea against obsession with age is based on present-day biological considerations. As I argued in my earlier book *Age and Vitality*, it is lack of challenge in the form of physical and mental activity which is far more likely to produce a decline of powers in later years than the passage of time itself. It is obviously impossible to stop or reverse the passage of time, but it is possible to adjust our attitudes and our mode of life in such a way that we help ourselves to stay fit and lively-minded throughout our life. This way of looking at ageing removes the sense of the hopeless, inevitable and irreversible decline of our health and strength.

Biological considerations

Modern research in biology and in medicine has shown, and is showing, that a living organism does not start life with a parcel of resources and energy which has to last throughout its life, and hence has to be used sparingly, especially later in life, lest the organism is left with nothing. The idea that the body is a machine has led to the dangerous concept that our bodies 'wear out with use'. They do not! They become stagnant, below par, and malfunctioning *without use*. The resources of the body are renewed, its energy is replenished and its proper healthy functioning is maintained *only* because the body is used. If animals are experimentally immobilised they function poorly, and many die after a limited period of restricted mobility. Half an hour a day running about in a large cage protects them from much of the harm of immobility. Most significantly, it is the *old* animals which suffer the greatest ill-effects from such immobility. In other words, to stay well older animals *need* sufficient physical activity even more than do young animals. Such findings suggest an emphatic contradiction of the advice often given to older people: 'Take it easy' or 'Do not exert yourself' or 'Take plenty of rest'. Rest from what? Rest after some effort is necessary because during such rest the body actually replenishes its resources. But rest after inactivity is merely stagnation. Most unfortunately we describe two completely different states by the same word 'tired'. 'Tiredness' after exertion is a healthy feeling, and is removed by a period of rest. 'Tiredness' from boredom, immobility or mental torpor, is an entirely different thing and rest does not remedy it.

The benefits of physical activity are not confined to strengthening our muscles, our co-ordination, and our sense of balance, but spread to the whole of our metabolism. That is the reason why these days people are made to move about as soon as possible after surgery or after some acute illness. Prolonged bed rest may lead to all sorts of complications. In good geriatric practice prolonged bed rest is looked upon as a danger to the patient, and is therefore prescribed only in exceptional cases. It is easier to nurse patients who are neatly tucked up in bed, but this is not medically sound if the patients are to return to health and independence as soon as possible.

Physical activity and our attitudes to old age

What has physical activity to do with our attitudes to old age? It has a great deal to do with it. If we banish the preconceived idea that exertion is somehow unnatural or dangerous in later years, because it may use up too much of our store of energy and so undermine our health, we shall then stop watching our step *because* of our *age*. Instead we shall be free to carry on doing whatever we may wish to do, provided we feel no ill-effects from it. We shall also be encouraged to look after our health sensibly, and not to accept aches and pains as 'normal for our age'. Since physical challenge is positively good for us we may proceed sensibly and gently, doing a little more rather than a little less as time goes on, and so becoming fitter. This is possible in old age. Some studies on people in their sixties showed that, over a period of ten years, none of these people, who followed a programme of physical exercise – sport, rambling, swimming, and similar activities – actually suffered any decline or deterioration. In fact they all improved their performance and in effect were fitter and 'younger' physiologically in their seventies than they had been in their sixties. And these were ordinary people, not life-long athletes.

It is unfortunate that the trend of modern life steers us towards less and less activity in our daily living. This affects all of us, including children, adversely. We are not as fit as we should be and this makes us more vulnerable to the hostile factors in our environment. Admittedly, great epidemics do not ravage the developed countries and famine does not reduce our numbers. Instead, our numbers are reduced by degenerative diseases which afflict the less fit among us. To be fit is important because fitness is a protection against any threat that may arise and which may lead to ill-health. It is natural for us to assume that the way we live is 'normal' for us. It may be so, but it is not often optimal. If we walked more, or climbed stairs more, or did more gardening, and so on, we would be fitter and would age better. In some ways human inertia is perhaps the most powerful force that governs our lives. Yet the price exacted by inertia is precisely what we all fear about old age: it leads to eventual ill-health, to loss of faculties, and to dependence. Fewer of us would suffer these ills provided we exerted ourselves beforehand, to help ourselves remain fit.

The dangers of inactivity

None of us in our right mind would dream of taking a small, daily dose of a slow-acting, cumulative poison like arsenic, and of making quite sure that we increase the dosage as time goes on. Chronic and increasing lack of physical activity and of mental stimulation is also a slow-acting, cumulative poison. Total immobilisation of a fractured limb for several weeks renders it weak and useless, until exercise and *use* restore its function. Nobody is surprised at this. Small doses of immobility, which increase as we grow older and which are imposed on us through inertia, laziness, or a misguided belief that one may overstrain oneself – these do not produce such dramatic effects. But they act in a cumulative way – they weaken our muscles, our nervous co-ordination, all our functions are insidiously impaired. Even before we reach calendar old age we become progressively out of condition and we present, in time, the classical picture of an old person: slow, listless, stiff-moving, and more and more immobile. In later years our bones may become thinner. It is not age alone which makes them so, it is also the loss of calcium from bones when the muscles of the body are not used. Such thin bones fracture more easily; lack of exercise also produces impaired nervous and muscular co-ordination and this results in a decreased ability to save ourselves from falling if we happen to trip or stumble. Fortunately, being out of condition is a state which can be reversed – at any age – by sensible and gradual training.

Our image of the pattern of human life

The popular image of the pattern of human life is that the time of development is childhood. Well, obviously childhood is the time of growth and development and of many new challenges. Middle life is envisaged as the 'prime of life' – but is it? It may indeed be a very busy period, but at the same time it may be very confined and the person as a whole may develop very little. Too much time, attention and thought may be channelled into too narrow a course: career, child-rearing, running a home. In time, when these preoccupations recede, very little may be left to give content to our lives. It is then that the popular image of old age may indeed apply and we may be justified in seeing it as a dwindling, empty and unhappy time of life. But this is not the result of some biological and inevitable change in *us* with *age*. It is the result of our mode of life, of the challenges we face or shirk or avoid, of the demands we make or do not make upon ourselves as human beings. As with physical activity, so with mental activity, it is possible to develop mentally at any age, and the more we use our minds and senses the better they will function. Since the body and the mind are inextricably interrelated – not only metaphysically, but actually biochemically – an active body helps the mind as much as an active mind helps the body. The best insurance for a verdant 'old age' is provided by a mode of life which encourages suppleness of body and flexibility of mind. This premise should serve as the foundation for our concern for older people in our midst.

2
Good Health in Later Years

Expectations

Good health is obviously so important at every stage of life that there is no need to labour the point. Our attitude to good health in later years often follows the same unfortunate trend as our attitude to our mental abilities or physical fitness: we expect them to decline *because* we are getting older. There is no need to expect any such decline to be natural. Decline does occur, but mostly because we expect it to occur. We expect that in time life will be diminished in all its aspects, and we do nothing positive to prevent or to remedy this state of affairs. It is much more natural that we can and should be in good health at any age, provided we live sensibly, enjoyably and expect to be well. Then if we do not feel well at any time we should seek the *cause*, and not ascribe our ill-health to our age.

The idea that we cannot possibly be physiologically strong and well at seventy or eighty or ninety is so ingrained, so much a part of our subconscious, that even people who are seventy or eighty or ninety, and *objectively* very fit and healthy, may still have an uneasy thought, from time to time, that it is somehow not *natural* to be so well. They may dwell on some minor deviation from health, or begin to fear some disability that might develop. These feelings derive from an obsession with thinking of age first, and only then of one's actual state of health or fitness. Those older people who do not suffer from stereotyped images of age do not waste their life in a state of suspended animation, waiting for things to become worse simply because time is marching on.

Practical points

(a) *Health checks.* Health checks from time to time are good sense for people of any age. An early recognition of a heart complaint, of anaemia, of diabetes, of clinical depression, of even perhaps the ill-effects of still taking some drug which is no longer necessary, may prevent much ill-health.

General practitioners are not yet fully accustomed to the notion that their older patients may require them to give advice on how to keep healthy and fit. Doctors are disease-oriented in their training and in their practice. This means that they treat disease rather than watch over the health of their patients. In ancient China a physician used to be paid so long as his patient was well, but not when he fell ill, for the physician's duty was seen to be to keep his patient's health from deteriorating. There was wisdom in this arrangement. The climate of opinion is changing now as to what old age should be like for most of us, and so health surveillance, timely advice, and prevention as well as cure, are emerging as desirable measures for the well-being of the elderly. This of course is the sort of approach which was applied earlier this century to the problems of child health and welfare and which was responsible for the great improvement in both over the years.

Perhaps if more elderly patients were to ask their doctors to give them a check-up, and then to advise them on what positive health measures should be taken concerning such matters as nutrition, exercise, and mental activity, the general practitioners might begin to see themselves as health educators and advisers as well as people who treat disease. Older people should not feel that they are trespassing on a doctor's time if they wish to be instructed in how to keep fitter and healthier: they are saving his time in the future. Moreover, National Health practitioners are paid a larger fee for their patients aged over sixty-five than for younger patients on their list. A recent survey showed that surprisingly few people are aware of this fact.

Taking sensible care of our health does not make hypochondriacs of us. Any acute disturbance or the persistence of some symptom or discomfort in an otherwise reasonably healthy person needs medical attention. We all occasionally have headaches, which soon pass off, or respond to an aspirin, but if the headache is still there the next day, and the next, it is time to see a doctor about it. Similarly, if we have over-indulged and spend an uncomfortable night because of an upset tummy, there is no reason normally to do anything except to eat sparingly the next day. But if after every normal meal we feel uncomfortable over a period of time, we should attend to this. It may be a digestive trouble, it may be a psychosomatic, but it should be cleared up. It is not a result of getting older.

Older people should not put up with being told: 'What can you expect? You are not getting any younger.' As I said before, expectations tend to fulfil themselves. So you should expect to be well, *and your doctor should expect you to be well*. If you are not well, then it is not a normal state of affairs, however old you are, and it is the doctor's job to put things right.

Illnesses and disabilities do, unfortunately, accompany old age – but they are not, in some magical way, caused by it. This distinction is important. My point about health in later years is summed up by the case of a lady of ninety who was listless and very weak. Fortunately she was seen by a doctor who did not dismiss her state of health as being due to her great age and therefore 'natural'. He examined her, diagnosed anaemia, prescribed the right treatment, and now at ninety-seven this same person is full of life.

(b) *Mobility*. Aches and pains in joints and muscles are perhaps the discomforts most frequently ascribed to approaching old age. More likely, they are the result of our mode of life. It is always advisable to make sure that the pain is not caused by rheumatoid arthritis and this can be done by having a simple blood test. If you are anxious to preserve your mobility then you have to heed your doctor's words about exercise. In most cases he will advise it. With any exercise, always start gently, but have in mind that to keep fit you should try to do progressively a little more, and you will then in time achieve fitness.

Any condition which makes walking painful should be attended to. Trivial complaints such as ingrowing toe nails, bunions or corns can in time reduce an active person to a housebound one. Reduced mobility is a real threat to good health. Even chair-bound or bed-ridden people should be encouraged and coaxed to move regularly and as much as possible whatever part of their body is mobile so as to protect them from general deterioration. It is *not* natural for people to need less and less movement as they grow older. Immobility is only natural for those who are dead.

(c) *Hearing and vision*. If your hearing or your eyesight give you trouble the usual advice is that you should seek help and acquire a hearing aid or spectacles. Of course you should. But a hearing aid may present some problems. It may take some time to get used to hearing again a great deal of background noise, which people with normal hearing find a nuisance, and which you may have in fact been spared for some time. It may not always be easy to adjust the volume of the aid correctly. But whatever problems may arise, it is worthwhile to persist using a hearing aid and not to withdraw from contact with others. For if you withdraw, not only do you hear less, you also listen less – and listening is an essential part of communication. When people mumble, or speak with their faces out of your sight, you may succeed in understanding them better if you tell them that you cannot hear very well, and would they mind making an effort to be clearer, because you are *interested* in talking to them. This will flatter them, they will feel that they have something interesting to say, and chances are they will make an effort – if only temporarily. If you simply say that you cannot hear well and could they speak up, this may make them feel a failure, they would be likely to resent this, and they may make very little extra effort.

Having acquired the right hearing aid or spectacles, and having got used to wearing them – what is the next thing to do to get more out of life? To ensure that you have something worthwhile to listen to and to look at! Try to extend your experience. If you love music, go to concerts. If you are interested in politics, or languages, or whatever, join a class, listen to the radio, start a discussion group. Learn a craft; or teach a craft you know to others. Read some books which are different from the ones you have read in the past. Do something new. When you are out, look at the world around you rather than simply straight ahead; and listen to the sounds of life.

(d) *Dentures.* Well-fitting dentures are essential for proper nutrition, for morale and for the aesthetic impression we make on others.

(e) *Some hazards.* For mobility to be encouraged, the home should be made as safe as possible. Since more accidents happen at home than anywhere else, *every* home should be made as safe as possible. Obvious things like poor lighting on stairs, rugs on slippery floors, torn or rucked-up carpets – anything on which a person can trip – should be seen to. Awkwardly placed switches, mirrors above fire-places, faulty electrical wiring in old houses, uneven steps, slippery floors in bathrooms and lavatories, all present risks.

Medicines kept in unlabelled or inadequately labelled containers are a great danger. All medicines should be clearly labelled with the name of the drug and with the condition for which it is to be taken. For example: ' "Mogadon" – sleeping tablets' tells you exactly what the medicine is and why you take it. A label which says 'The tablets – take one at night,' *is not safely labelled.*

There is another risk with medicines. People tend to go on taking a drug long after the need for it is gone. This may happen with sleeping tablets. If such tablets are taken over a long period, long after the specific reason, such as some pain or an emotional upset, for their prescription has disappeared, unpleasant side-effects may result. For instance, a patient who was in hospital for a few days because of a skin complaint was given two sleeping tablets every night, to enable him to sleep in spite of unfamiliar surroundings and the noise in the street outside. He went home, and since his wife had the same sleeping tablets in the house, prescribed for her some time previously, he continued taking two of her tablets every night. After several months of this regimen, he became uncertain on his feet, very drowsy during the day, and eventually even mentally confused. When this drug was stopped, his symptoms disappeared. It is common practice in geriatric hospitals to take newly admitted patients off all drugs. Not infrequently, the patients need little other treatment, and are allowed home after a short while with their often alarming symptoms entirely gone.

Outside the home, traffic presents the greatest hazard to all of us. People who do not hear well should be especially careful to watch out before crossing roads, for they often cannot hear a vehicle approach.

Another risk which many of us may face at some time has to be added to this short list of possible hazards. The risk lies in our inability to sort out whether we are physically ill, and therefore feel depressed, or whether we are suffering from clinical depression and therefore feel ill. If everything seems too much for us, if we feel apathetic, inert, unable to pull ourselves together, or if we feel that everyone and everything around us is threatened by some formless dangers – then we need help. In such circumstances we are not likely to have the will to go and seek help, and it will be up to our families or friends to encourage us to do this. If that is the case, we should let them arrange for help to be given us: these days clinical depression can be successfully treated with various medicines. Depression is prevalent among older people who have retired, suffered a bereavement, or have some other problems, but it is not often recognised for what it is by the person suffering from it. Here again it is too often taken to be a sign of 'old age' – but it is *not*!

PART II
Family Situations

3
A 'Ground-plan' of Family Situations

If we are trying to describe a house to someone, it is much easier to do if we draw a sketch of the ground plan for them, so that they can visualise the size and relationship of the various rooms, the situation of the windows, doors and so on. We are not showing them the actual house, with all its concrete detail and its particular atmosphere, but we do make it more real than by just describing it in words. In the following pages I am similarly sketching a ground-plan, as it were, in discussing in general terms some of the more prevalent types of family situations in which older people may be involved.

The inner emotional content and climate of any family is unique, because it is created by the particular personalities involved, in particular circumstances. And yet each type of family situation has a general configuration, some general features and relationships, which can be discussed and which can help to clarify the issues.

Within every mode of life, ranging from living alone to living within an extended family of perhaps three generations, it is possible to ensure maximum well-being and continued vigour for older persons. It is worthwhile from every point of view, including that of crass self-interest, to try and achieve this aim. Success in this direction is easier to attain if members of the older and of the younger generation each jealously guard against two cardinal sins. The older people should try to banish any tendency towards self-pity and to combat mental rigidity. The younger ones should also try to banish any tendency towards self-pity or towards self-sacrificial martyrdom and they should curb the need for proving that they are children no longer.

The 'generation gap' is a man-made problem. One generation intermingles with the one ahead of it and with the one behind – they all live, day-to-day, in the same world. They have, of course, a different amount of experience of this world, they view it from different points in time, but there is no natural gap. The man-made gap is produced because we are too lazy, too inarticulate, or too frightened to bridge it – because we think first of our age, of our stereotyped role within the family and within our society. We do not think enough about people as people, about ourselves and about members of our families or of our community as just human beings, who have the world about us to share.

People who are kind or amusing, interested or sweet-natured or knowledgeable, are intrinsically worthwhile – their age, or their place within any particular generation, does not matter. When a person tells you that she is not at all interested in younger people because 'All they want to talk about is themselves, and they don't want to listen to what I have to say' – what do you conclude? That the speaker is really interested only in herself? It is not a matter of a generation gap here, but of self-centredness.

People often talk of the generation gap, and in the same breath, of how grandparents and grandchildren often get on better together than either does with the middle generation. Since the time gap is obviously greater between the grandparents and the grandchildren than between either and the parents, what really matters here is the stance of each generation *vis-à-vis* the others. The parents have a management job to do, so to speak, and in doing it they may be either too authoritarian, or too lax, or too anxious and insecure. But the two outer generations can get along well because they may meet on a more direct, a less stereotyped, basis.

The roles we play within the family are obviously important, but they should not be regarded as immutable, by us or by our families. We come face to face here with a need for flexibility – a quality which perhaps more than any other ensures continued vitality.

Some types of family situations
(a) *An older married couple.* Among older married couples there exists a whole range of possible relationships: from the idyllic one, when the two people have always been 'on the same wavelength', who have built a long life together and who continue living it with zest and in harmony; to the most unfortunate situation when each partner seems bent on destroying the other, not in fact but in spirit.

The common factor in all cases is that the two people are still a human and social unit – whether a happy or an unhappy one, but at least a familiar one. Their view of themselves has not had to change, they have not had to attach a different label to themselves. Their mode of life, their possessions, their circle of friends are there to reassure them about their identity. If they have not been happy together, but have not separated by the time they have been married for thirty or forty years, then their need of each other or of their 'unit' is likely to be greater than any possible advantages which they might sometimes wish for themselves as separate beings.

Whatever the quality of a long-standing marriage, the younger members of the family can, and should, supply refreshment for the older couple. Not cloying care or duty-motivated interference, but an involvement in at least some aspects of their lives, a chance for the older people to be aware of the current problems and joys which face their younger relatives. This will expand the older couple's horizons, and prevent them from becoming preoccupied with the past, and limited and boring to themselves as well as to their families. It will also make the younger people feel closer to them.

(b) *An independent, unmarried older person.* Here again there is a whole range of possibilities: from a person who had always led an active life, gathered a great number of friends, god-children or colleagues, and who continues living a full and contributing life; to the inward-looking, self-pitying person who feels, and is, alone. The former needs no help. The latter does, but is neither likely to seek it, nor to be given it spontaneously, because where self-pity exists sympathy from the outside vanishes.

An unmarried person living independently needs to adjust to nobody. If one lives with a relative, or friend, adjustments are of course necessary, and will have been made. As time goes on, it becomes important to remind oneself that the other person will *need* to preserve his or her identity, to make decisions, to have an independent opinion, and one should therefore not be restrictive or over-protective. Even if one had been used to arranging everything oneself, one should, in later life especially, encourage others to take some independent action – for two reasons. Firstly, to promote their better physical and mental health, and secondly, to enable them to face life more courageously should they be left alone at some future time.

(c) *A widowed person.* The loss of a partner is all the harder for many people because of the practical readjustments which become necessary. The sense of loss is then increased by the change in familiar surroundings, by the dissolution of the long-lasting 'unit', by the need, perhaps, of giving up a house and moving in with children or relatives, or facing the prospect of living alone.

Whatever the quality of a marriage, bereavement is a sorrow, a shock, and a loss. If it was a happy marriage, then the partner is missed and yearned for. If it was unhappy, there will be a sense of perhaps remorse, or guilt, or regret. Whatever the reaction of the widowed person, the situation is a very difficult one, and unfortunately it is just then that readjustments have to be made. Here the relatives or friends have a most important part to play. They have to show kindness and *understanding*, to let a person alone for a while if that is what they wish, to let them weep and grieve if that helps them, or to encourage them to take a grip on themselves and plunge into some activity, if that is likely to bring them relief. Depression is very common at such a time and often it is best to encourage the bereaved person to seek medical help, rather than to trust to time alone to heal it.

A particular difficulty which I have in mind is this. Supposing a recently widowed mother is asked by her loving and caring married child to come and live with the family. A person who is depressed and distressed is not in the best frame of mind or condition of spirit to integrate easily and happily with a group of people. So what was kindly meant, and gratefully accepted, may start off badly, and generate all manner of feelings of resentment. The mother may perhaps come to feel that the family are not sufficiently considerate towards her, and the family may feel that they have failed to make the mother really welcome or happy with them. A pattern of unsatisfactory relationships and reactions may thus emerge and progress. The importance of realising clearly that any bereaved person needs careful, thoughtful handling – for a time – and a gentle bringing into the normal stream of life thus becomes evident.

Any invitation to a bereaved person to come and live with a family or a friend should be issued in two parts, as it were: a period of looking after in the way best suited to the bereaved person's needs, followed by a gradual integration into the normal life led by the family or friend. This should be clear – and spelled out – in the minds of those who invite, and understood by the person being invited. Another thing which should be clearly realised is that a person left without a partner should not be expected to – and will not – lose his or her personal identity. So if we talk of integration it must not be assumed that the invited person should do all the integrating. The group will now include him or her, and *everyone* will have to readjust to this new situation. A person invited out of pity, or out of a sense of duty, and then resented for not gratefully submerging himself or herself in the group, is treated neither fairly nor kindly. Some readjustments on everyone's part are necessary simply because good relationships within any group are no more made in heaven than are good marriages.

(d) *A daughter's family.* Theoretically, coming to live with a daughter's family should be perhaps the happiest arrangement, insofar as the key relationship here is between people who have known one another all their lives. In practice, it may indeed work out very well, or it may founder on the very thing that should ensure its success. To many people it is extremely difficult to accept that someone they raised from babyhood has become a mature person in her own right. This may be especially so when a daughter, in her middle years, has of necessity a good deal of management to do. This may make her appear too much of a 'boss' to her parent(s) and lead to resentment. Her particular way of bringing up children, for example, may be criticised without her possibly being asked *why* she does it like that. Here flexibility of ideas, flexibility of approach to roles within the family, and mutual respect of person for person are all needed.

Often relationships within a family are moulded more by the

wife than by the husband. Then it is up to the daughter to do her best and to ensure that her parent(s) and her husband take a mutually positive attitude towards each other.

(e) *A son's family*. To make a success of coming into a son's family, one has to be lucky in the son's choice of a wife. There is no life-long familiarity here between the parent(s) and the person with whom they will possibly have more actual contact than with their son. There will not be the common background of earlier years, of milieu, or quite simply of love. All this may bring difficulties and need a great deal of dedicated beavering away at making the arrangement a success, on *everyone's* part. On the other hand it may, in a sense, be a help, that one is unlikely to regard one's daughter-in-law as still a child.

(f) *Grandparents and grandchildren*. The presence of grandchildren in an extended family household can be a wonderful boon – or a bone of contention. If it is the latter, the situation is often blamed on the grandparents, on their old-fashioned ideas or on their interfering ways. To my mind, grandchildren become a bone of contention when the parents have views about bringing them up which are too rigid. Such parents do not seem to realise that the adults in the two generations have *different* things to offer to the children. Moreover, grandparents have a degree of detachment from immediate and direct responsibilities for the bringing-up, education, daily needs, etc. of the grandchildren. This leaves them free to provide an easier contact with the grandchildren than may be possible for the parents to achieve. Grandparents have more time, more experience, and often a greater sense of proportion which allows them to see priorities in better perspective. It falls to the busy parents to drill good table manners into a child, but a grandfather's more leisurely life may allow him to instil into his grandchild a love of poetry, or a sense of wonder at nature, or the delight at making things with one's hands. Children cannot but profit from realising that different people have different ways. If they absorb this in the context of family life, in the contacts with adults who wish them well, who love them and are interested in them, then they have a far better chance of adapting well to the world outside, with all its diversities and complexities. They are more likely then to develop that flexibility of mind which is so vital and helpful at all ages.

Of course there is need for consistency in some aspects of life; and no child will thrive on being treated like a yo-yo by parents and grandparents *as a way of life*. But an occasional variation of routine, and the recognition that a particular person has particular ways, are a good thing. When an important issue is at stake, for example whether an adopted child should or should not be told about his adoption – a frank discussion of the problem should be held, and a consistent line of action agreed upon by all the adults involved in the family group. But a trivial issue, such as whether a child is given a bath before, or after, an evening meal is not likely to make a dithering neurotic of him in later life. Such flexibility may teach him that he can contribute to the convenience of others by slightly altering his own habits.

(g) *Roles within a family group.* It may sound a somewhat artificial thing to discuss roles within a family, for this phrase may conjure up some kind of play-acting, a self-conscious assumption of an image, or even of posturing. In the present context 'roles' refer simply to the way people interact within a family group. It is the mother's role to bear the children; it is the father's role to take a part in their bringing-up; it is the grandparents' role to give the grandchildren some loving attention and interest, and so on. Ideally, all members of a family group should give willingly, and receive gracefully. In practice, some of the people may do so some of the time – more or less – because of their natures, their expectations, their circumstances and experience. The important thing, as so often, is to be clear in one's own mind and to make clear to others, what role is desired in any given situation. There is no need to be brutal about making one's desires clear, but there is need to be firm.

An extraordinary and almost instinctive attitude seems to exist that 'old people' should be *grateful* for being accepted at all into an extended family, on any, even most unsuitable, conditions. To do one's duty by one's older relatives, and then to blight their lives by taking it out on them in thought or in deed, is neither kind nor fair. Would we not all condemn people who took in a child: and then deprived it of love or of material comforts? We would not consider that the child should be grateful for *any* crumb given it – we would feel that the child needed, and had a right to, love and attention in order to thrive. But this need and this right exist at all ages. Older relatives, dutifully 'cared for' in an unloving atmosphere, will not thrive. Equally, not every older person has the same needs. A frail, dependent person may wish for, and thrive on, being looked after, pampered, and cosseted. It would be wise for this to be made clear, however, *before* coming to live within a family group. Such a person should make the effort to say: 'I've lived a long life, I have done a great deal; now I wish to enjoy being taken care of, and I shall thrive on it.' Another person, active and independent in spirit, will be diminished and demoralised by being treated like an honorary family pet. Here again it would be best to spell it out: 'I have lived a long time and I still enjoy being myself, doing things for myself – and for others – so please do not prevent me from playing an active part in life.' A man, recently seen on television, who had retired late, and presumably had been more active than the average, was now living with a married daughter's family. Both the daughter and her husband spoke with shining pride and pleasure about 'taking care of him' – they saw to it that there was nothing the father needed to do for himself. But the older man's remark was revealing. He said there was nothing for him to do on getting up in the morning but to wait for bedtime. A shattering thought. In this instance, both the father and the children had acted according to stereotyped notions of what a retired man should do, and of what a loving child should do for him. If the father had been told beforehand, 'All you need to do now is to get up in the morning and wait for bedtime,' he would never have accepted such a prospect willingly.

Perpetual daylight, perpetual spring may be lovely in theory – but it is the succession of night and day, and of the seasons, which really gives shape and spice to our lives. The provision of opportunities for a 'change of seasons' in the life of older relatives, is essential for their true well-being.

PART III
Attitudes Within the Family

4
Older Persons' Attitudes

Person or child?

Members of a family see one another at very close range and often this prevents them from really understanding or evaluating what sort of *people* their relatives are. In speaking of a member of the family, especially of grown-up children, we usually say 'My daughter is very capable' or 'My son is reliable' and not 'My daughter is a very capable woman' or 'My son is a reliable man'. We do not really acknowledge that our daughter or our son is a mature person in their own right, acting in an independent capacity.

It may be argued that there is nothing wrong or unnatural in continuing to regard one's son or daughter primarily as a child. But for a mutually satisfying relationship to grow and develop a son or a daughter should be regarded as a *person* even in baby-hood, let alone in maturity or even comparative old age. To continue thinking of a mature man or woman as a child and to treat them accordingly may indicate two things. If one is ego-centric one may really love a child primarily because it is a part of oneself, an extension of oneself. No need is then felt to alter one's attitude to one's children throughout their lives, and they are loved because they are one's offspring. Another situation may occur when a parent has, actually, a profound lack of interest in the child as a person in his or her own right, and therefore fails to form any opinion of the grown-up son or daughter, on his or her own merits. Both these situations deny the younger person's fundamental need to be loved and appreciated by the parents for what he or she is as a person at any given time. Possessive or egocentric parents with such attitudes sometimes fear and resent anything and anyone that enters the lives of their children which they feel may threaten to alienate the children from them, or to divert their interest or loyalty. But somewhere between smothering possessiveness and resigned withdrawal there lies a life-enhancing, spontaneous, and warm relationship between parents and children. In this they are close to one another not because of bonds, but because of a natural gravitation to one another which provides comfort and enrichment for both.

What will be the likely effects produced by the persistence in treating a grown-up son or daughter as a child? A person of any spirit at all is likely to resent a denial of maturity simply because of a difference of generation. This resentment may take the form of over-assertiveness, or of excessive touchiness, or of sulky moodiness. The younger person will then insist on proving that he 'is a big boy now'. One way or another these effects are likely to make even ordinary contacts difficult. If as a result the parent feels hard done by, neglected, or hurt, it may help to reflect a little, to come to terms with the reality that their child *is* a mature person or one who craves to be recognised as such by his parents. It is a test of our own maturity if we can bring ourselves to make such a reassessment. Grown-up people, sometimes even without admitting it to themselves in so many words, do tacitly crave the approval and appreciation of their parents. If this is not expressed, much warmth can evaporate from the relationship; and not only warmth but mutual enrichment.

Resentment of the 'management' generation
Another parental attitude which may develop is the tendency to think of the grown-up children as 'they', the 'management class'.

At their stage of life the 'children' are so occupied with careers, the raising of a family, the building up of social contacts, that they have to manage a great many things. A mother in a three-generation family, for example, needs to know exactly which day of the week the children have a scouts' meeting, when the window-cleaner will call, who of the family needs to have a dental appointment made, whose clothes need mending. She is, of necessity, well oriented about the activities and timetables of the family. If the grandparents are not in any way involved in these activities, and are not perhaps even informed about them, their life will lack a framework and they may then feel themselves relegated to the status of children who have few responsibilities or duties. A fairly passive person may find this situation irksome, but be unable to mount enough opposition, and so will gradually become disoriented when decisions are being taken by the 'managing' members of the family, plans are made by them, or arrangements are seen to by them. This sort of disorientation is also a depersonalisation – it diminishes an individual and saps confidence and initiative. A more active person will be irritated and affronted by any signs of being taken over by the 'managing' members of the family. Depending on the temperaments and personalities involved, the resultant difficulties and frictions may assume many guises, but whatever form they take, each side will be the loser. The children may feel that their best-intentioned care is spurned or insufficiently appreciated, and the parents may either fume in frustration or enter into open strife. Dependence of any sort brings in its wake a feeling of insecurity. If the props are removed, there is no confidence that one's own resources will suffice. Of course very often they do suffice, but one is unwilling to test the situation, and much time and energy may be wasted in worrying about eventualities which could put one's resources to the test. For instance, a grandmother living with her daughter's family but not normally involved with looking after the grandchildren, dreaded the prospect of doing so whilst the daughter was away for several weeks. But once the daughter set off, the challenge was there, there was nobody else to fall back on, and no difficulty was encountered. In fact, the grandmother not only managed splendidly, she enjoyed the experience and relished the feeling of regained self-confidence. Older people prize their independence; in any situation threatening their independence it is to their advantage to make a stand – through co-operation rather than confrontation, if possible – and to put forward their case as clearly and openly as they can. More will be said about this in Chapter 5.

Unwillingness to keep up with developments
Yet another attitude which tends to build a wall and isolate an older member of a family is his or her unwillingness to become informed, to show an interest in new developments or in present-day ways. For example, how often do we hear someone say something like 'My son-in-law is something in computers; I don't understand it, of course; we did not have anything like that in my day'? Every statement in those sentences is a little citadel, isolating the speaker from his relative, from a field of knowledge, and from a very important feature of modern life. He is clearly not sufficiently interested in his son-in-law as a person to have bothered to find out *what* it is that he does 'in computers'. He shuts his mind even to the possibility of assimilating *some* information about computers and acquiring a glimmer of understanding. He excuses this lack by the irrelevant fact that computers did not exist 'in his day' – but today is still *his* day, since he is alive! Anything to do with modern life, with the concerns and interests of the younger generation is *not* automatically unintelligible to older people. They may show a lack of interest, or even hostility towards modern life, but there is nothing so mysterious or removed from human experience in

our world today that older people, given the information, the interest and the wish to understand, could not make part of their world too. They do not have to like it all, or approve of it all, or even really understand it all in depth. Opportunities for building closer and more rewarding relationships are missed for want of a spark of *genuine* interest in another person's life, not because of disparities of age.

Tendency to proffer criticism and advice

It is so easy to criticise and to give advice – but what is the result? More often than not it is a defensive reaction from the younger person, a justification of actions or motives. In a family where the grandchildren spend a lot of time watching television, for example, a grandparent may express disapproval of the fact, and suggest to the mother that it may be interfering with their studies. The mother is very likely to reply that her children watch no more than other people's and that it is very difficult to regulate the amount of watching they do, and anyway they would feel 'out of it' if their friends discussed programmes which they could not watch. In this case the mother is defending the existing situation instead of simply saying 'Yes, I am rather concerned about it myself' or 'They are doing well at school, so it is not doing them any harm to watch as much as they do.' The impulse to justify oneself in this case often stems from a reluctance to appear wanting in wisdom or ability in the parent's eyes. It is not a very clever way to establish one's worth in the parent's mind, but more of a 'gut reaction' and, as such, likely to lead to further conflict rather than resolve any difficulties.

The importance of words

Too often the parent whose advice or criticisms are rejected feels that there is automatic contradiction to, and automatic rejection of, everything he or she says. Perhaps the feeling that it is *automatic* reflects the response to a stereotyped approach on the parent's part. Instead of saying 'Why don't you do it this way?' it may be more rewarding to say sometimes 'Tell me, why do you do it like that?' The first question implies that the other person's way is somehow unsuitable (implied criticism, to a sensitive recipient's mind); the second question asks for information (a sign of overt interest). The key words are 'tell me'. It may seem trivial to rephrase a question, but the words we use are signals which do not only impinge on our minds but also on our 'gut reaction centres', whatever they may be. We form habits of speech, and use words without being aware at times what effect they have on others. A man who says 'surely' at the beginning of a sentence often makes others bristle just because of this dogmatic word. Some people have an emphatic or a highly colourful way of putting things, and even a trivial topic raised by them may provoke a reaction quite out of proportion to the content of what they are saying. There are words which we all use and which are fraught with danger when they are not used literally but for emphasis, e.g. 'never', 'always', 'everybody'. 'People never tell me anything'; 'I am always wrong'; 'Everybody is against me' are the sort of things we say – and get little sympathy in return.

At this point the reader may well say 'Good heavens, must I re-learn how to speak to my own children?' No, if we are happy with our relationships, then we are fortunate and all is well. If we are not happy, then a little effort with semantics may well be worthwhile. It should not be a reflection on us, or on our children, that a familiar way of speaking to one another may need a bit of revision or adjustment. If we burn the toast to cinders every morning, then it is sensible to adjust the heat or the timing. It would be futile to rush out and buy a different *kind* of bread, and proceed to leave it at red heat for ten minutes. Similarly, we do not need to change ourselves, or our relatives, to improve our relationship with them – adjusting the signals we give them is a far more realistic way of achieving the end we desire. It is not only older people who may benefit from modifying the signals they emit. A young mother can drive a toddler into a welter of agonising decision-making by constantly putting questions to him about actions which are a foregone conclusion in her own mind – 'Shall we put your pyjamas on?', when putting him to bed, obviously not intending to let him sleep either naked or in his jeans and sweater. Bed-time could well become more peaceful if the mother tried saying 'Let's put your pyjamas on'. These words would be more honest, and they would let the child out of a decision-making effort devoid of any real choice.

The trouble with words is that they are so very important, and at the same time they are in such constant use, that this very familiarity with them breeds contempt for the need to use them properly. Words can be understood literally or metaphorically, they can be used directly or deviously, they can build resistances or open all doors before us. There is no need to bother if our interactions with people are positive, rewarding and easy. If they are not, it may be an interesting exercise to take note for a while of just how we put things to people as a matter of habit. Admittedly, changing our habits is difficult but not impossible, especially if these habits lead us into difficulties, or produce reactions, which we do not enjoy.

I have heard it claimed that in their need for having *some* sort of relationship with others, the need for *some* sort of response from others, there are people who will put up with, or even provoke, inconsiderate, unkind, quarrelsome, or other beastly behaviour towards themselves. This may well happen, but it seems to me to belong to an area of warped emotional needs which do not exist in the majority of people to any pronounced degree.

Communication and communion

What I have said so far revolves around the need for good communication, which helps to define our own views and wishes, and which can bring co-operation and harmony into our lives. Most of us, however, need communion as well as communication with the world around us. So many of the world's ills, and of individual unhappiness and frustration, are considered to be due to a 'lack of communication'. This has become almost a catch-phrase. There is much truth in the idea that if we do not communicate effectively we are likely to be confronted with difficulties, and with missed opportunities for improving our relationships or our circumstances.

Communication is a two-way process: it is an exchange of information, a mutual clarification of ideas, feelings or reactions. *Effective* communication is a *selective* process. It is, ideally, illumined by clarity, graced by concern for, and interest in, others, and enlivened by enthusiasm. It may be deliberately slanted in such a way as to produce the results we want. It is *not* an outpouring of the total content of our minds at any given moment.

On a personal level, communication is often hedged in by reticences or reluctances to reveal all, and this often happens especially among people who are close to one another. This may be so because we naturally care that those close to us should think the best of us. In communication we *select* what we reveal, sometimes consciously, sometimes subconsciously, perhaps out of concern and respect for another person's feelings, perhaps for our own advantage, perhaps because of innate shyness or because we are inarticulate. Such selectivity in what we communicate is a reflection of the innate and profound privacy of life. In the final analysis each one of us is a totally private world. We really know people around us, even those closest to us, only as the 'images' of them which we have in our minds. Total revelation of anything is unnatural. Our senses and our mental equipment take in, process and retain only a minute fraction of everything which impinges on us, and discard everything else. The innumerable processes of life going on within our own bodies, within the plant and animal life around us, go on in silence and out of our sight. We are organised in such a way that our beings are focused on as much as we can cope with of all the immensity of space and time. In a sense, each human being is a model of perfect packaging, physically and mentally. Our skin is the frontier between 'us' and the universe. Within it our tissues and organs, the contents of our bodies and of our minds, are marvellously packaged, with things kept apart or brought into contact, as the need arises – immensely busy and yet so insulated from our consciousness, that we are not disturbed by the tremendous activity going on within us.

This digression on the privacy of life is prompted by a thought that with so much talk about the need for communication we may perhaps be too anxious that we do not communicate enough. Communication is, of course, essential because nobody can exist and function well in a vacuum. But there is no need for a feverish pursuit of communication, or of too much 'baring of the soul'. Communication does enrich life, because it brings us the reactions of others, news, information; it helps us to shape our lives, to sharpen our wits, to form opinions, and so on. But there is another way of enriching our lives – through communion.

Communion is a far more private process, one-way and undemanding. Essentially, I suppose, when we commune with anything or anyone we immerse ourselves in the experience: and we absorb from it an enrichment of the senses or of the spirit. We may commune with nature by watching the clouds, which are silent and totally unaware of us. By listening to bird-song again we may commune with nature, although we are quite unable to 'communicate' with the singer in our own language, or to understand the message of the song. The sheer delight of the sound serves to enrich us. Music and art in all its forms and the fruits of human thought, or simply the presence of particular people, can all provide us with the experience of communing. We all know the feeling that all is right with the world if a particular member of the family is at home. Just being under the same roof, with each person occupied in their own way, can contribute to a feeling of communion. This has a bearing on how we feel within a family: there is no need to feel neglected or excluded if members of the family do not spend hours chatting with us. If we feel slighted by a lack of communication we may withdraw into ourselves, and so miss the opportunity of communion.

To give a workaday example: when a member of the family comes home after a tiring day, a sense of communion is more likely to be generated by greeting him with 'It is good to have you home!' and then pausing to allow him to unwind, rather than by saying 'Hello, did you have a good day? Are you tired? Would you like a cup of tea?' We state our pleasure at seeing him come home, and then leave him be for a few minutes to readjust himself, instead of demanding instant communication from him, of news, state of health, and his wishes. This example brings us back to the need for proper choice in the use of words, for such choice really reflects an attitude. If we are primarily concerned for the *other* person's comfort and ease, we will attend first to his need for welcome and peace. If we are primarily concerned for *our* needs we will confront him with queries, choices, etc., because we feel *we* need communication. It is likely that after a little peaceful interlude we shall have this need satisfied with more news communicated to us by a willing person than we would manage to drag out of a tired person the moment the threshold was crossed.

In advocating a primary concern for the other person I am

not in the least advocating humility at all costs on the part of an older member of the family group. I am advocating self-interest, and a way of going about things which is more likely to produce the reactions from others which we hope for and enjoy.

Particular dangers

There are two important things to beware of. Self-pity is the first, and perhaps it is the real cause of most of our troubles. Self-pity should be pulled out from our lives by the roots, like a noxious weed. Sir Lawrence Bragg once said that if one hoped for sympathy from other people one should not indulge in self-pity – if you pity yourself, nobody else will.

The second danger is putting labels on ourselves, on other people, and on situations. Labelling is a dramatic device which may make mountains out of molehills. For example if we think of ourselves primarily as a 'teenager', or a 'housewife', or a 'mother', we then tend to give one aspect of our lives an unwarranted dominance, which obscures the complexity of our beings, and the potential richness of our existence. In itself this situation may not be so serious, except when the label we wear in our mind is one which has diminishing or, worse still, pathetic, connotations. A man who has worked, and is now retired, does not help himself to feel a valid human being by harping on being 'an old age pensioner' in his own thoughts or in his conversation. A woman who has had the misfortune of losing her husband and thinks and speaks of herself as a 'widow' creates a pathetic impression which reflects self-pity rather than the fact that she is continuing her life as herself, but in altered and sadder circumstances because of her loss.

The need for dramatising ourselves is perhaps more basic and widespread than we think. Perhaps this need arises from a wish to make our lives less dull, less colourless. But unless the greyness of our lives is really stultifying, it seems to me that dramatising ourselves negates a directness in our relationships with the world and with people. Dramatisation makes us think and act more 'for effect' than because we really *need* to act in a particular way, or are *moved* to do so by an actual inner drive. For example, if we think of ourselves as 'helpful neighbours' we may visit a lonely person, making sure that our friends know about it and appreciate our action. However, if we do not think of ourselves in any special way, but think of this lonely person who needs a bit of companionship, we simply visit, but do not make a point of mentioning the fact to anybody outside. Similarly, there is a difference between starting to attend a course in a foreign language because we decide that we would like to learn it, and starting to attend because we like to be regarded as a 'person with outside interests'.

In these two examples of a direct relationship the first one concerns only the lonely person and the visitor and the second only the student and the acquisition of a foreign language. It is a one-to-one relationship in each case, and a more telling one at that, whereas in the dramatising situation there is always a three-cornered involvement; the subject, the object and the audience. Even performing artists, who of necessity have an audience, achieve real greatness only when they are most directly involved with their particular art, be it music or the projection of a character in a play. They permit, as it were, the audience to witness the result of their direct relationship with the composer's or the author's creation. The presence of the audience does, of course, impinge on the performing artist in this situation, but not as the prime mover of the performance. Performances 'for effect' may be exciting, thrilling, brilliant – but I doubt that they are ever great. A virtuoso is not always a profound musician.

It is a remarkable fact that among those people who have lived a long time, but who remain fully alive, this directness, this one-to-one relationship with life, is very prevalent. They are not given to labelling themselves as anything, although they could do so easily enough, having done a great many things and filled a great many roles in their lives.

The habit of attaching labels to oneself, or to one's situation, is directly related to a tendency to be egocentric. And that is where the danger lies: whether egocentricity results in megalomania or in a morass of self-pity, it never attracts anybody's sympathy or interest, those reactions for which the egocentric person craves. It would be naïve to advocate that an egocentric person should analyse the motives of his behaviour, and change himself into another human being. But if we are aware in ourselves of a tendency, however slight, towards egocentricity, towards labelling ourselves, and above all towards self-pity, it would repay us to make an effort to check this tendency.

5
The Managing Generation

In this chapter, as elsewhere in the book, the younger people and the older people referred to are those of us who are on the whole reasonably fit, reasonably comfortable, who are not invalids, who are not overwhelmed by personal or social difficulties. This has to be made clear for two reasons: first, most people *are* reasonably all right most of the time; second, just because they are not in any dire predicament does not mean that these people do not merit some thought and some encouragement to make their life and relationships more rewarding.

The attitudes which are discussed here are those involved in the fabric of daily living; they are those which form our general view of the older person, and of the needs and welfare of that person. In a crisis situation most of us discover strengths and resources in ourselves which we never suspected we had, and we cope. It is not a crisis but day-to-day living which is likely to tax our patience or blunt our understanding of another person. This happens because we drift from one day to the next, we drift into situations and relationships which may be unsatisfactory; and if nothing happens to jolt us into taking a fresh look at them, we remain enmeshed.

In most cases our attitudes are made up of many elements

present in differing proportions. In this chapter I shall discuss some of these elements individually.

Neglect
At the two extremes of the whole range of possible attitudes of a younger person to an older member of the family lie gross neglect and utter devotion. It is easy but not helpful to moralise about such cases of neglect. The underlying reasons must be very deeply rooted in conflicts, incompatibilities, grievances, defects of character or pressures of circumstances of a magnitude which is outside the limits of ordinary human experience. Neglect is an appalling problem, but fortunately it does not arise for the vast majority of us. Most elderly people who have a family do have contacts with them, which may be more or less happy, more or less satisfying, but which in any case are real. And yet the component of neglect may exist in many relationships to a varying degree. It then results in more or less deprivation, but not in total isolation of the older person.

If we neglect to inform our older relatives about our activities or plans, if we neglect to inquire about *theirs*, if we pay them formal visits which produce no more than the most superficial contact, if we allow them no part in our lives – then their life is deprived of a chance of expansion. This may happen because we find ourselves to be incompatible with the older relative. It may happen because we are too wrapped up in the activities of our own life. It may be because we are afraid of giving an inch of ourselves, for fear that an ell will be required next. We may be over-jealous of our independence and assert it by keeping others isolated from any real contact with us. Whatever the reason for any degree of neglect, it reflects some incompatibility, or some human inadequacy in ourselves, some difficulty in making ourselves available from time to time to another human being in a direct and interested way. Our existence is often illumined by the light radiated from another's life – and for older people very often it is a member of the family who can best serve as the source of such light. If contact is not invited by the younger person, the older one is likely to turn inwards and perhaps even pretend not to be interested in the world outside. The notion of such 'disengagement' – the wish to live in a shrinking world of familiar things, and to withdraw from life – is an artefact. It is a phenomenon which we do observe; but it is not dictated by any biological laws of ageing. It is far more likely the result of not wanting to chance rejection. It is a defence mechanism, a means of self-preservation from hurt.

Neglect or deprivation breed insecurity which in turn breeds isolation. People who feel insecure, who are on the defensive, tend to be unattractive, whether their feelings of insecurity make them aggressive, or make them a pathetic figure to the world. This applies, of course, to younger people just as much as to the older ones: an aggressively 'independent' grown-up child may indeed inspire a 'disengagement' wish in an elderly parent! The idea that disengagement is a natural development with advancing years provides a comfortable excuse for those among us who do not bother to make the effort to involve older people. This disengagement theory also serves as the basis for those appalling institutions – the segregated communities of retired people which exist in various parts of the world.

There is no instant remedy for any degree of neglect by a younger member of a family. The nub of the matter, as always, is the need to *think*. It requires a real effort of will and of understanding to think oneself into the situation of another person, but it may bring rewards by transforming a dull, formal relationship into one with some interest or warmth in it. Older people respond as readily as anyone else to a more positive approach or to a livelier contact. So it is worth trying.

Devoted care

It may seem a paradox that in discussing devoted care for an elderly relative by a younger person I stress, as I stressed in considering neglect, the need to think oneself into the other person's situation. It may be asked: 'If there is devoted care, what else is necessary?' And the answer is that what is also necessary is true concern that the older person has every opportunity to retain his individuality as a mature adult.

Without in any way at all questioning that devoted care may be motivated by love, respect, kindness, loyalty and a wish to make life as good as possible for an older person, we have to question whether such care is always in the best interests of the very person for whom we are caring. The word 'care' implies that an active person looks after a passive one – and the adjectives hold the answer to our question. If, as we have seen earlier, it is activity which really helps us to live well and to age well, then being taken care of, being passive, is not in the best interests of anyone who is ageing or elderly. We have to make a conscious effort to understand this, for all our instincts and all our cultural and ethical teachings bid us to 'take care of', to 'look after' our elders. But in former times our elders may have been broken by excessive toil, may have been infirm, and unlikely to have financial independence – and filial devotion then did mean the provision of hard-earned rest for the aged. A retired parent these days is not likely at sixty-five to be a man broken in health and spirit – and what he needs on retirement are outlets for his often considerable resources of energy. He needs to develop these resources and not to have them atrophy through lack of use. A woman of sixty-five nowadays often has more go in her than her daughter, or even her granddaughter in some cases.

Let us take a hypothetical case of a widowed mother coming to live with a daughter's family. Assuming what is normally re-garded as the best possible conditions, where the older person is genuinely loved, where she has always had close contact with her daughter's family, where the relationships within the family are warm and easy, here the very abundance of love and care may in the long run blur the older person's individuality. When someone comes into a family at a time when her own resources are depleted because of bereavement, the natural response of the family is to lavish love and attention on her, to save her trouble and to protect her from effort and the strain of decision-making. This is what the widowed person needs at that particular period of time. After a while the family can say with genuine satisfaction: 'Mother does not need to lift a finger, or bother her head about anything. We are only too glad to do everything for her!' But what has become of that human being who happens to be the mother of this particular daughter? From a contributor to life she has become a consumer of care. From someone who has lived a long time in a direct relationship with the world about her, she has come to be insulated from the world through the agency of other people. Does this matter? Of course it does! No adult will thrive in body, mind and spirit if their independent control of their own lives even on a trivial basis is diminished. A natural support for all our systems of body and of mind is an active life, and older people are far more robust, and far less different from the rest of us, than we have become used to thinking. So in the case we are considering here, after the initial period of nursing Mother through her loss, it is kinder to her, and better for her, as an *individual*, if her family gently begin to involve her in doing things for herself, in making decisions for herself, in discussing *their* problems with her. All this will help her to establish that she exists in her own right, and has the ability and the opportunity to live according to her own lights. The surest way to kill vitality is to frustrate every possibility of physical or mental exertion. Over-protection eventually breeds insecurity, for with everything being done for one, self-reliance and self-confidence are stifled and decline will follow. Decline is the last thing a loving and caring daughter would wish for her mother, and yet she may be in danger of producing it by her very devotion and care. It is a real danger, and it can be avoided by tempering filial emotion with some clear thinking about its unintentional effects.

Care dictated by convenience

Let us consider another hypothetical case, of a widowed parent coming to live with a daughter or a son, whether single or married. Again, in the initial period, it may be necessary to protect the parent from physical and mental stresses. Such care, initially prompted by genuine kindness, may grow into a habit, simply because it is quicker and easier to do things for the parent in a household which is perhaps a busy one, or a well-organised one. It may indeed be convenient to persist with such an arrangement, but it will not benefit the older person.

Inviting an older person into one's home is a responsibility far greater than taking in a pet. Human beings need to continue existing in their own right, and to have a sphere of influence, a feeling that they remain in charge of their own life, even though they may have to share it with their family. The extent to which duties and responsibilities are shared must depend on health, strength and gifts rather than on age. The duties may be something as physically untaxing as arranging flowers, if a person is frail, or driving the children to school, if Granny is a driver, or digging the garden, if Grandpa is fit and strong. The crucial point is being *responsible* for a particular job. If the 'managing generation' involved in such a situation finds it unacceptable to share out any responsibilities and chores, then it would have been kinder to spell out the problem at the outset. The parent should have been told that a temporary stay would be fine, but a permanent arrangement in such a tightly organised household would leave too little independence for the older person. Harsh advice for a harsh situation, if the younger people involved have organised their life so inflexibly that there is no real place in it for another human being of full stature.

In cases of care dictated by convenience, not only is independence eroded, but involvement is denied too. So the older person misses out on both counts. It may indeed be more convenient to bring Granny her breakfast in bed every morning, and it may even make her feel spoiled. But if she happens to be an early riser by inclination or habit, it might be of more benefit to *her* to make the breakfast for the family. She would certainly feel more involved and useful.

Over-anxious care

Unless there is real ill-health, or a disability, in older people there is no reason to hover over them, fearing that they might 'overdo it', or even – horror of horrors – forget their age, and launch into something new or enterprising! To do a little more rather than a lot less is the healthy way to live, and it is healthy for people at any age. All persons of any given age do not possess equal gifts, abilities, or motivation. Hence some succeed better than others in various undertakings. In later years encouragement is increasingly important for an older person to try something new, or to be a little more ambitious. It is this kind of encouragement which is missing when care is over-protective.

Patronising care

Care for our elders is patronising care if it is tinged with an expectation of gratitude. A younger person expecting gratitude assumes, however subconsciously, that the older relative is somehow inferior or less important. From this assumption of superiority, which may be totally unfounded, it is only too easy to slip into patronising ways of speech or attitude. Most people are sensitive about being patronised and resent it. It is not therefore likely that an easy and mutually enhancing relationship will develop between the patronising and the patronised.

The 'managing generation' may feel superior because they are in the mainstream of life, they know about current events, they use 'in' words, they are familiar with today's personalities, whilst an older member of the family may not be so well informed. But lack of information can be rectified – today's events, trends and personalities can be discussed with an older person – their ability to absorb information is not lost, and their curiosity can be roused. Do we at times subconsciously hug this superiority to ourselves, not wishing to share our knowledge or store of information and so to keep this edge we have on our elders?

Another example may be found in a family where the 'managing generation' has had a better education, or has achieved a higher professional or social position, than the parents. The lack of ease and the degree of patronising which creep here into the inter-generation relationship, are often in direct proportion to feelings of insecurity on the part of the younger people. It is sobering to realise, however, that most people who get on in life, and who overtake their elders in education or in achievement, do so partly through their own gifts and hard work, but partly also because they were able to stand on the shoulders of the previous generation.

Dutiful care
A strong sense of duty is an admirable quality but not always one which generates ease or warmth in human relationships. It may be that an older person is materially better off, because a younger relative provides financial support or food and shelter out of a sense of duty towards this person. But spiritually there may be little comfort, or opportunity for enrichment, in this situation.

Fortunately, a sense of duty may be tempered by courtesy, by concern, or even at times by sympathy, and it is then not likely to be allied to a patronising attitude. Martyrdom is a likelier companion to a strong sense of duty for the latter may lead to too heavy a burden being carried. A daughter, for example, may take on more than she is actually able to cope with – either because of her circumstances or her personality – and then self-pity will begin to seep in and resentment against the older person will build up. A person who allows herself (it seems to be mostly women who are so afflicted, perhaps because both traditionally and actually they fill a 'caring' role in the family, and have fewer commitments outside the home) to be imposed upon, and to become a martyr, is in an intrinsically difficult situation. It seems to me that such a person has an urge to be needed to such a degree that it is satisfied only by allowing another human being to become demanding and to expect to be served. But there is a further twist here: the martyr may feel overwhelmed by the demands, but at the same time she also exercises immense power over a person who has become by now utterly dependent on her in some aspect of life. The scene is thus set for resentment on *both* sides, which may be contained in an uneasy peace, or break out into open hostility. There is probably no remedy for this situation, because one of the strongest characteristics of a martyr is the refusal to take any steps which might alter the status quo and provide some relief. It is a sad state of affairs, because one person spends her life in caring for another but in a resentful, sometimes almost a harsh, way – with perhaps only an occasional glimmer of warmth or of humour.

Heavy-handed care

When an older person is very important to a younger one – perhaps as an 'anchor' in life, or as someone whose presence and influence have illumined and warmed the younger one's existence, then care is given gladly and devotedly. This certainly does enable the older person to retain full stature. It is unfortunate that in some cases, just because of the importance of the relationship, the younger person tends to over-react. For instance, a complaint about a headache may trigger off some anxiety, and the urging of a visit to the doctor. A chance remark about present-day education may lead to a full-scale tirade from the younger person defending the choice of schooling for the children. People like that have not, perhaps, an innate lightness of touch, or the ability to let go, to laugh things off. It would be worthwhile here to cultivate a lighter approach, a lighter reaction. Basically such heavy-handed responses may arise from two causes, a wish to be approved of by the older person, and a dread of losing either this person or his or her love and esteem. A case of emotional immaturity, perhaps. Such a personal prism may distort what is often a splendid relationship and preclude an easier, more mature exchange of thoughts and views.

Insecurity so often bedevils relationships. Reasons for feelings of insecurity may be legion, but the net result is the same: the need for reassurance, for approval, and for reiterated expressions of both. If this need exists, then any criticism, real, implied or even imagined, voiced for example by a parent, is likely to be taken badly. A flare-up of temper, argumentativeness, being on the defensive, aggressiveness – all these unpleasant reactions may be rooted in feelings of insecurity within the younger person.

It may not be easy, or even possible, to sort out what the reasons for feelings of insecurity may be. But if we examine and think about our reactions we may recognise that insecurity is responsible for some of them. It may then be possible to say to a parent: 'Look, you are important to me and your approval is important to me! Every time I get on a high horse talking to you, it is because I am trying to defend myself from the feeling that I am not good enough for you, and I could not bear that. I know it sounds potty, but there it is!'

Another aspect of insecurity is the tendency to take things personally when they are not meant personally. After all, other people's worlds do not revolve around oneself, so that the thoughts, views or opinions they express are meant generally, more often than not. It is an arrogance to ascribe to others an enveloping preoccupation with oneself.

Muddled thinking

Sometimes a person can take a step without really thinking it through, and thus create both an unfortunate relationship and an unfortunate situation. Even at the risk of being repetitious it is impossible to stress enough the need for clear thinking about others, before we involve them and ourselves in some permanent fashion.

To illustrate this, let me recount briefly an experience described by a lady some months ago in a national newspaper, and analyse some of the points in it which produced the result she deplored. This lady, married to a teacher and with a family of eleven children, decided that since her father and her stepmother were now in their eighties, they should come to live with her. The older couple duly moved from their home 300 miles away, and came to occupy the room made available to them in their daughter's home. Since the two households had been so far apart geographically there was not much close contact between the people involved. The lady's father had been a merchant seaman before he retired; he had lived by the sea in his own home, and had gone daily for long walks along the sea front. He enjoyed meeting his old friends in a local pub. The family had looked forward to having the grandparents come, but it soon became clear that the older couple were not really happy, the father having nothing whatever to do all day, and the stepmother spending her afternoons and evenings watching television (and spilling her beer, or her stout, on the living room carpet!). The grandchildren were treated like errand-boys or servants, bewailed the daughter, they could no longer have their friends over for pop-music sessions, and the daughter herself had no chance to spend a quiet hour talking to her husband. Life had become hell on earth for everyone, with the daughter bitterly resenting the intrusion of the grandparents, and their lack of gratitude and graciousness.

I may be wide of the mark in surmising what went wrong, since I do not know personally the people involved in this unhappy story. But even so, several things are clear. The whole enterprise was based on muddled thinking and the idea which initiated it was wrong-headed. The fact that the grandparents reached a particular *age* triggered the daughter's decision to uproot them. Age, calendar age, of itself is *no* reason for taking any drastic action, and she should have gone to visit them, seen for herself whether they were reasonably fit, ascertained what local services and help could be called upon, in case of illness or need, and discussed with the older people themselves what *they* really wanted to do: to stay where their roots were or to come to her into a family of thirteen. It is this sentimental idea that older people are automatically happier within a family, however remote from the family and their way of life they may be, which often prompts such major upheavals. The daughter also obviously did not in fact think about her father and her stepmother as real people at all: they were figureheads to her. She was doing what a good and dutiful and decent daughter should do. The whole family had not really thought about these two newcomers as real people either, and resented it when the elderly couple did not obligingly merge into the wallpaper, but proved to have habits, tastes and manners which were unacceptable to the rest of the family. The daughter seemingly never mentioned

– and possibly never gave it a thought – whether the older couple had any views on the eleven children into whose midst they were thrust. It was apparently assumed that the older people would do all the adjusting, and the rest of the family would go on as before, with just a little less room for them in the house, and loads of approbation for having taken the old people in. But these old people would have been far better off left in their own home, among their own friends, where their interests and habits and occupations did not upset anyone. The daughter took precipitous action to forestall a possible crisis, should illness or accident occur. But is it worth it to forestall a hypothetical crisis, at the cost of condemning two people to years of living as unwelcome and resented intruders? If they have spirit enough *not* to submerge without trace in a family of thirteen assorted people, then they have enough capacity to live their own lives in their own home.

A sin, a pitfall and an arch-enemy

The cardinal sin against older people is to refer to *age* as the root cause of any diminution of mental or physical ability, or as the *reason* for allowing oneself to do less and less. I do not, of course, advocate that everyone who has reached retirement age should be driven to work in the saltmines, or set to learn the London telephone directory by heart. But nobody has the right to say 'You are too old to try' or 'You should not continue doing this at your age' – or even to imply it. If we really care for our elders who are reasonably fit, we should dread hearing them say 'I don't go to the library *any more*' or 'I've stopped doing the garden *now that I'm getting on*'. If they say it, we should take it upon ourselves to discuss with them why they have stopped doing this or that, and to encourage them not to limit their activities. They may have got fed up with the unhelpful librarian, or got discouraged by a poor showing of flowers, and simply used their age as an excuse for stopping a particular activity. There is little wrong with that, but there is everything wrong with age being the reason for contracting, for jettisoning something, without a fresh interest or involvement taking its place.

Once we understand the fact – and it is a fact – that people of a particular age, whatever that age may be, whether it is nineteen or ninety, differ in their abilities, gifts, personalities and experiences we are less likely to take over an older person's life simply because they have reached a particular age bracket. If Grandma has never dealt with bills in her life, of course it is kind and helpful for a member of her family, or a friend, to do it for her – or, better still, with her. But if Grandma has managed a business all her life there is absolutely no excuse for the impertinence of offering to do her bills for her once she has reached retirement age.

The main pitfall for all of us, young and old, is the conditioning that makes us equate old age with universal physical and mental decline. If we get rid of this notion, a whole new prospect of older people continuing to live actively and hopefully opens up before us. This will allow people to live without being cramped and blighted by the idea that nothing new, exciting, stimulating or joyful *can* happen to someone who has lived a long time. This does not mean living in a fool's paradise where no illnesses, no accidents or unpleasantnesses ever happen; it simply puts these into perspective, as occurrences rather than as the fabric of life in later years.

The arch-enemy of a younger person, as of an older one, is self-pity, for it blinds us to the needs of others and blocks our understanding of another person's viewpoint. Perhaps the best remedy against self-pity is to realise that its indulgence is an admission of inadequacy and of self-centredness. If we dislike the thought of ourselves as inadequate self-centred beings, then we can either try and shed some of our burdens, or better still try and carry these burdens in a different spirit. There are people who carry intolerable loads, and who suffer under them, but who do so without self-pity. Self-pity is not, after all, synonymous with suffering.

6

Why an Older Person May Be 'Difficult'

A reader may think 'It is all very well to preach that we should think about the older person all the time, but what about *me* who have to cope with a difficult older relative?' It is a fair question, but the answer is still that the best way we can help *ourselves* in dealing with a 'difficult' older person, is to think about that person and try to find out why he or she is difficult. It is the only way to get down to causes, and thinking about ourselves and *our* burden will not do that. Considering our *own* plight can produce a positive result only if, on carefully thinking the problem through from *our* point of view, we can bring ourselves to pass the burden on to somebody else and to feel cheerful about it. If we pass the burden on and feel guilty about it, then nothing good has been achieved.

When we say that a person is 'difficult' we may be referring to a number of things. It may be that a person is unco-operative, or cantankerous, or irritable, or glum, or apathetic, or demanding. These characteristics are not exclusive to older people, and older persons are most likely to be, basically, the same in later years as they had been all their life. A gentle and considerate person will become a gentle and considerate older person; a self-centred, demanding one will become a self-centred and demanding older one. Our characteristics may become somewhat exaggerated as we go on, but it is unlikely that we change our essential nature simply because we grow older. This means that we should not expect an older person to act out of character.

Compatibility

The basic components making a person 'difficult' are that person's character and personality, the circumstances of his or her life, and the elusive factor of compatibility which colours relationships. The same person may react quite differently to different people, responding positively to some and negatively to others. Such affinity, or lack of it, is difficult to define, but plain to see. Compatibility is more a question of personalities than of character. Someone of sterling qualities, but with a buttoned-up personality, may get far less response than perhaps a less 'worthy' but more cheerful and open person. This may produce some bitterness, understandably enough, but it is not altogether surprising. We do not live on a profound level all the time, and sterling qualities are often revealed only in serious circumstances, whilst a cheerful word can light up any ordinary activity or exchange. Deep emotional involvement also does not always ensure compatibility. Because we expect a great deal from such a relationship trivial shortcomings in it make us question its deeper security. Feelings of insecurity make people react badly, and become 'difficult'. To illustrate this point let us consider the case I have come across, of a person who had a great need of affection, and also a need to dominate members of her family. When her attempts at domination were checked or rebuffed, she was hurt and offended. She felt that she was not loved or esteemed by her family. A particular incident may have been quite trivial – something like her insisting that people switch off lights, or wrap up warmly on a winter's day. This person never ceased to be surprised that she got on so much better with outsiders, who respected her opinions, who were kind to her, and with whom she felt so much happier than with her family. In fact, of course, she interacted with outsiders on a much less emotionally involved level, over limited periods of time, with no inflated expectations of what these relationships should be like. It was sad for all concerned that the sterling qualities which were there could contribute so little to any ease or warmth of family relationships, and that the emotional involvement made the exchanges of everyday living difficult.

Need for adjustment

Since so much of life is taken up by everyday exchanges we tend perhaps to underestimate how demanding they are. We can get along with almost any human being on a superficial and very short-term basis. But day in, day out contact often makes every difference and deficiency stand out more and more. It is simply unrealistic to put a group of people together, and to expect them to blend into a happy unit without any adjustment on anyone's part. Equally unrealistic is to think that it is the *other* person who should always adjust to *us*. To make any arrangement work, it is necessary to realise without resentment the need for mutual adjustments and readjustments.

Emotions which poison life

There are many older people who are well, happy, busy and active and who have no difficulties in their relationships with others. There are some emotions or states of mind which are extremely potent poisons; they destroy serenity, vitality and joy, if they are allowed to engulf anyone. Fear, boredom, and frustration are such poisons, and a most important task in our contact with older people is to try and banish or reduce these toxic components of their life.

Fear

Underlying fear may express itself in many ways: in anger, in irritability, in depression. Whatever expression it takes fear casts a shadow on the inner world of a human being. If one takes the traditional view of ageing, then there is fear of decline which may hound an older person. This fear may be groundless, but if it exists then it is a reality for the person concerned. This particular fear of *inevitable* decline is so unnecessary, in the light of present-day psychological and biological evidence, that we should do all we can to dispel it where it exists.

The fear of losing one's spouse, or friends and relatives, as times goes on is understandable, but it too acts like a poison for it darkens one's life whilst those one is afraid of losing are still with one. I have never been able to understand the advice of the poet who said 'Look thy last on all things lovely' – it would not enhance my sensibilities to remind myself that I shall not last forever, it would simply make me morbid.

Much distress comes from a fear of some disabling condition which would lead to dependence on others. Here again it is not a universal fate which overtakes everyone at some magic age. If we realise, as we should on present evidence, that there is much we can do to foster health and independence in ourselves and in our older relatives, then this fear too can be exorcised. In this context it is worth mentioning that people who give advice through the media on health matters need to be very careful how they do it. The adviser too often discusses some symptom which applies to a particular condition, some heart disease for example, but fails to mention that this symptom may be caused by some other, much less alarming, condition – such as indigestion for instance. When this is not made clear people may worry unnecessarily about this particular symptom. It does not help matters that most times the advice to avoid worrying is also given, as then people begin to worry about worrying as well.

The fear of financial dependence on others is perhaps less widespread now than it used to be, with more people having some, even if inadequate, measure of financial help from pensions. But it still exists, and it is still very much our responsibility if we give any financial help to our older relatives, to do it with tact and kindness, unblemished by any hint of a patronising or of a burden-bravely-borne manner.

Fear, of course, is not something which haunts only elderly people. We have only to think of children who are afraid of the dark, of spotty-faced youths who fear that they will never get a girl-friend, or of 'managing-generation' men and women who fear being unable to compete with their juniors in careers or in personal attractiveness. But elderly people too often have too much time on their hands, too few responsibilities, and too few opportunities to employ their talents or skills. All this makes it easier for them to fall prey to their fears. They should not be blamed for it: fears are liable to well up in our minds when there is little to distract us from them. If we are honest with ourselves, and stop to think really hard about the reason for our short temper with the children, or an impassioned tirade against some political event, or a morose reaction to our friends, we shall more often than not realise that it is a disguise for some fear lurking at the back of our minds. We dislike the word 'fear' – in our ethic it is not done to be afraid – so we tend to use euphemisms like 'worry' or 'anxiety' or 'stress' instead. And yet, at times, it is helpful and salutary to admit openly to oneself, or to somebody else, that, yes, one is afraid. In dealing with 'difficult' older people it is sometimes best to ask directly, but kindly and quietly, 'Tell me, what is it that you are afraid of?' They may not tell you, but they may think about it and perhaps, by bringing a fear out into the forefront of their mind, they will succeed in overcoming it, or at least in bringing themselves to talk about it eventually.

One of the reasons why I feel dismayed by the negative image of old age still too often projected by the media is that it arouses fears not only in younger people but in the older ones as well. An image which presents old people as frail, helpless, dependent, miserable and lonely *because* they are old, poses a threat to those who are none of these things. It creates a fear almost like that of contagion, because most people do not want to be saddened or distressed by their human contacts. For example, older people are at times reluctant to go to a day centre because they think that they will become 'old' among all the other 'old people'. If they are encouraged to overcome their reluctance they soon realise that their fears were groundless, and they come to enjoy the amenities and opportunities provided by the centre. Once they meet the people who use the centre they realise that these people are *not* an aggregate of ills and miseries, but a bunch of human beings, some livelier, some quieter than others, who are not a threat to anyone's peace of mind.

It is an intriguing thought that whereas *real* causes for fear arise only rarely in a person's life, our inner world may be crowded with phantom fears. How often do any of us hear bullets whistling round our heads, or feel burning planks collapsing under our feet, or encounter flesh-eating wild beasts in our path, or have our infants snatched from us by some demented monster? Hardly ever. But many of us spend much of our lives fearing – or 'worrying about', as we prefer to call it – all sorts of things that *might* happen, be it ill-health, failure of one sort or another, loss of relatives, or of friends, loss of job, loss of status.

One wonders why phantom fears take such a grip on some of us. Could it possibly be that we use these fears as a superstitious sort of insurance against *real* calamities befalling us? Do we feel that if we make ourselves miserable enough by imagining *possible* disasters and upsets we shall be spared any *real* catastrophes? Or are such phantom fears simply the price we pay for the gift of imagination? 'The price we pay' – a phrase which betrays an ingrained belief that we have to pay with something nasty for every good thing we have – contains an ungenerous view of life which is likely to rob our joys of their radiance. The point of this digression on the general nature of fear is that we should be alert to the possibility that a 'difficult' person is very likely a frightened person. We cannot help such a person unless we understand this. Getting cross, or feeling martyred because our kindness is not appreciated, or because our care does not produce the contentment we feel it should produce, helps nobody.

Boredom

Boredom afflicts those of us who have not the inner resources to generate interests, occupations or pursuits, which would give our life point and shape. Boredom is not reprehensible, it is sad because it is, in effect, a waste of life. It is perhaps particularly sad when it overtakes someone who had been very active in some sphere, and because of being deeply involved in it, missed the time to develop his or her inner resources. Boredom can result from isolation and neglect, from a lack of contacts, and a lack of opportunities to become involved. It can also result from *too much* care lavished on an older person by a loving family. Leisure, rest, freedom from all care and responsibility, are enjoyable only when they alternate with activity, with effort, with challenges. If we strive to make them a permanent way of life, we run a great risk of arranging for our elders a boring, empty and unrewarding existence.

One of the unfortunate side-effects of boredom is the likelihood of developing hypochondria. Fears about health do lurk in most people's mind, but they are suppressed or ousted by the other activities of a normally busy life. When such activities diminish, some of us switch in to a mental listening post for symptoms. If we pick up any signals we tend to dwell on them, and then this preoccupation takes the place of occupation in our lives. I do not suggest that we do this consciously. We cannot live in a vacuum; so we manufacture some sort of content of life from materials which are always to hand: our selves, and the threat to our selves. The result is wretched – for ourselves and for those around us.

Another undesirable effect of boredom may be the development of petty grievances, of obsessional preoccupation with routine, of idle gossip and 'nosiness' about other people's affairs. We understand very well that a bored child is often a 'difficult' child, but we do not so readily think that a 'difficult' adult, or especially an older adult, is a bored one. Once again we come back to this outdated view which still persists: that older people's lives *naturally* contract, that their minds and spirits do not need stimulation or creative outlets. This just is not true, and circumstances which would bore any reasonably bright younger person would bore an older one just as much. There is also the element of the duration of a boring situation. Anyone can put up with a few hours or days of boredom. But a prospect of nothing much happening, and nothing much to do, for months and years ahead, is a very different thing. It is enough to make anyone feel thoroughly miserable and depressed. Those of us who are easily bored are, unfortunately, also more likely to be short of inner resources, so the advice to pull oneself together and *find* something to relieve our boredom is not very productive. What we need is active encouragement, an active offer of a choice of things to do – in other words our circumstances need to be made less boring by an outside agency, be it family or community.

Frustration

If we take frustration to mean a thwarting or baffling of effort, hope or wish, then it is easy to understand how it can poison life. There is nothing about feeling frustrated which is peculiar to older people – at some time or another we may all feel thwarted. At any age it is not a feeling we relish, and depending on our make-up and on our circumstances we fight against it either by becoming morose, or by lashing out at people, or at institutions, or ideas – in fact at anything at all – in an effort to release our tension. In our society, frustration comes in later years from many quarters: if we have not had enough education we cannot fill our time with sufficiently interesting things; if we have plenty of ideas we may not have access to anyone who will listen to them; if we have all sorts of interests, we may not have the money to indulge them. Even the experience of a life-time on an everyday level, such as running a home, may be pushed aside by a well-meaning younger relative who takes over and does everything for us. Many people who have worked all their lives, and are then compulsorily retired, may wish to go on working in their old job or in some quite other field. They are often frustrated because it is still very difficult to overcome the rigidities of our age-obsessed institutions. As with boredom, so with frustration – much of it happens because we still assume that it is somehow unnatural or unseemly, almost, for older people to need activity, interests, productive and meaningful occupation, or a chance to contribute to the family or to the community.

It is extraordinary that we do not see the grotesque futility of all the clamorous striving for 'a better start in life' for our children, or for tough-minded, independent maturity for young adults, when it is assumed that all the qualities we try to cultivate – maturity, liveliness, sound judgement, and, yes, even wisdom – are suddenly switched off on our reaching the age of retirement! It is especially grotesque to hold such a view when we are likely to have a quarter or a third of our life ahead of us after retirement. We are a work-oriented society, and so people lose their status and their worth when they retire from productive employment.

It is time now to think a little more deeply about the quality of a society in which a sixth (as now) or a quarter (as it will undoubtedly be) of its members have lost their worth as human beings through retirement. Families too should rethink the value of their older members. Keeping up with the latest trends in smart talk, or being in the thick of a rat-race, does not of itself confer any extra *quality* on those so engaged. It is often for the sake of the young children in the family that the links with the grandparents should be cherished and fostered; the over-busy, productively employed mum and dad are not always the best people to convey something of the lasting values and interests in life to their offspring. Parents may sometimes be better equipped and educated, technologically speaking, than the grandparents, but they may have a great deal less to offer in the way of serenity, or of a direct interest in some sphere of life, or of tolerance and interest in another person's (viz. child's) view of the world. The parents may even simply be much less interesting, because less experienced as people than the grandparents.

If older people we are dealing with are 'difficult', then it is very likely that they are feeling frustrated, especially if they are not 'cabbages' and if the circumstances of their lives have contracted. Frustration leads to resentment, and to bitterness and self-pity: all negative, unattractive emotions. If we try to understand that frustration lies at the root of such emotions, then we shall see that it is not the person who is unattractive to us, but the person's circumstances which are difficult.

Depression
If an older person seems listless, apathetic, gloomy and out of sorts or out of touch, we must *never* assume that it is just old age creeping up. It may well be depression – in the medical sense – and this needs medical attention. In lay terms, to be depressed often means to be in a bad mood, something which lasts a few

hours or days. But medical depression is a different matter, and if it is not attended to it can last for months, and make life very miserable indeed, particularly for the people suffering from it but also for those around them. It may not be easy to persuade a depressed person to seek medical advice, but it should be done. There are very effective and safe drugs available, and doctors are able to prescribe that which is the most suitable for a particular type of depression.

Circumstances which may be expected to produce an adverse reaction are a sudden change of life-style on retirement, moving away from a long-established home, bereavement, or financial worries. These may all make a person unhappy or sad or worried. But if such a natural reaction persists for a very long time, and nothing seems to alleviate it, then depression in the medical sense may well be present. Such depression, left without attention, may sap a person's strength and may make life seem scarcely worth living.

7
Voicing Anxieties and Problems

We may all have some anxieties at various times but we may either give voice to them occasionally, or often, or hardly ever. There are difficulties inherent both in excessively frequent voicing, and in 'bottling up' these emotions, and the difficulties exist both for the older and for the younger persons. For a start, the elderly do not have a monopoly on fears and anxieties. The 'management generation' may have them aplenty, though theirs may be of a somewhat different character. Without, however, going into any specific problems or anxieties, there are two central questions. If we are in contact with older persons who tend to keep quiet about their fears, should we encourage them to voice these? If we are dealing with people who are given to talking about their fears and anxieties, is it better to tell them to 'buck up' and curb their outpourings, or is it better to provide a safety valve for their inner pressures, and to listen to them?

'Bottling up' of any emotions does not banish them of course. It may save us from knowing about them, it may save us from being distressed or bored by another's anxieties, but it does not remove them from that person's mind. And in that mind these emotions may grow, and fester for lack of an airing. It may be difficult to get a reserved, private type of person to lay bare their troubles, and it would not be helpful to probe or to pry. It would be helpful, however, to try and make a conversational opening from time to time, to allow these troubles to be expressed. This may need an oblique approach: instead of saying 'Are you afraid of becoming bed-ridden?' for example, it may be better to mention how someone who *is* bed-ridden is still managing to get something out of life.

Anxieties can be of two kind: the 'real' kind of anxiety which is a response to some objectively threatening situation, such as an eviction notice, or an impending operation; and the 'ritual' kind of anxiety which seems almost to be a superstitious insurance against some real calamity. In this latter category come those anxieties about health which extraordinarily healthy older people sometimes have. 'Real' fears need real help if it is at all possible to give it. 'Ritual' fears need to be dispersed by reassurance given with a light touch.

A light touch is also essential in dealing with persons who do not keep their fears to themselves, but pour them out. It may be a bore and an irritation at times to listen to other people's reiterated anxieties, but we have to learn to react to them lightly and reassuringly, and not to dwell on them, by word or in thought. It is a pity that we do not realise how often people who do readily voice their troubles actually voice them at the moment that they think of them, and do not in fact spend their time nursing these worries. Those to whom they have talked may indeed be left with a worry for a long time, especially if the recipient of the voiced fears is the type of person who himself tends to bottle up his own fears. If both parties have a fair exchange about their troubles, then they understand how fleeting these troubles may be in the other's mind.

Because voicing of anxieties is a necessary safety valve, it is important to create an atmosphere in which no constraint is felt about discussing fears or problems. Over-reaction on our part is natural enough, when someone close to us seems to be burdened with many fears, but it is unhelpful. Our over-reaction really reflects our *own* unvoiced fears that something may be threatening the well-being of this person we love. And it effectively deters this very person from again confiding in us, as we seem to find this upsetting. The more important person in this case is the one who has fears, and we should see this situation in proportion, and our role in it. It is more important to provide a safety valve than to cushion ourselves from a passing upset. There is self-interest in this too: if voicing a fear helps our older relatives to feel better, to get reassurance and comfort, then it will make them brighter, less inward perhaps – and we shall find it easier and more pleasant to be with them.

In conclusion, there is a small practical point which may be helpful. When some morbid topic has been trotted out yet once again, and discussed for a little while, we may – and indeed should – let it go and turn the conversation to something else. It is then that we should resist the temptation to say 'Let's talk about something more cheerful now!' This sort of remark is likely to produce an immediate conversational vacuum, and a feeling of unease. If we really feel it is time to talk about something else, then it is up to us simply to change to a more cheerful topic ourselves.

8
A Boring Person

It is not only old people who may be boring to others. A schoolboy, who has no other conversation except monosyllabic
answers to questions, is just as boring as a garrulous old man
recounting trivial episodes from his past, or a dedicated money-
maker who thinks, talks and dreams of nothing but money.
There may be several reasons why we tend perhaps to object
more to an elderly bore than to a younger one. A boring school-
child is mercifully at school for a large part of the day. A boring
businessman is at his office all day, and very likely brings some
of his work home. We therefore do not have to put up with these
bores for much of the day. But an elderly person who happens to
be boring may be living with us and is at home all the time –
there may be little relief. On top of that, we may have an ambi-
valent view of elderly people. In one sense we rather expect that
anyone who has had a long life should have developed some
interests and acquired varied experience. We therefore resent it
when they do not seem to have done so. In another sense we
may dismiss older people as relics of the past, who have nothing
to contribute to the present, and who have nothing worthwhile to
say about it. Both notions brutally oversimplify the situation.

As I mentioned before, people do not change radically as they
grow older. A boring schoolboy is likely to grow up into a

boring adult, and carry on being a bore to the end of his days. But if a lively adult becomes a boring older person, then there must be a reason for it. Some people are able to generate liveliness because they have inner resources of intellect, or of personality, or of heart. These people are very fortunate and their life is evergreen. Other people will maintain liveliness in *response* to their contact with others and to their environment. When these conditions change for one reason or another then their liveliness may fade.

Before we prejudge an older person as a bore, it is as well to try and find out whether he or she was ever lively and interested in the past. If not, then it may be a very difficult job indeed to inject some fresh ideas or interests into this person. In the case of those who had formerly been lively, however, we should take a look at the present content of their lives, and compare it with that in the past. This should give us a clue, for when the present content is small, the horizons will contract, and a person will have little left to respond to with any spirit. The result will be a boring human being.

Older people do not need to grow less bright or less able with age: they retain potential for developing interests, and pursuing activities, old and new. But this potential has to be realised, and the necessary first step is to encourage older people to 'have a go'. Nobody will respond positively to a categorical statement that they are expected to do this or that. A call for help, or praise, elicit a response much more readily. We are more likely to involve older persons in some community project, for example, if we tell them that we are short of people who can help. We are even more likely to succeed, if we say that we are short of people who can help *and* who are as good with people or as clever with their hands, or whatever, as they are.

Boredom often starts when some absorbing, long-followed way of life is altered. For example, a man who has retired from a job which has no follow-up interests built into it, may have had little time whilst working to develop other interests. When the morning arrives on which he no longer has to go to work, he may greatly enjoy his freedom. But several mornings later he may feel completely at a loose end. He may fill his day with desultory reading, watching television, pottering about – but all these pursuits are not enough to make a life full, or to provide opportunities to develop in any way, or even to acquire fresh topics for conversation. After some time spent like this a man will become boring, not because he has reached the age of retirement, but because his life has become boring.

Another important thing is that one should always try to assess the merit of a person according to one's *own* views, rather than to take somebody else's opinion of them. To illustrate this point, when a young occupational therapist came to work in a hospital ward, she was told not to bother to involve an old man of ninety-odd in the corner bed. He was very deaf, and it was not worthwhile spending time on getting him to join in. This young woman, however, watched the old gentleman for a while, and noticed that he was spending a good deal of time writing something. She took the trouble to find out, and discovered that he had a most lively interest in, and a tremendous knowledge of, the history of the particular area of Norfolk from which he came. He was writing up some notes on this, to pass the time. The therapist was most impressed by the man, and spoke about him to various people. Before long a lot of people became involved, newspapermen, photographers, local residents who were interested in the history of their area – and the old gentleman had become the centre of it all. It needed one person's independent, alert and sympathetic attitude to transform an isolated, boring existence into life.

The classical image of a boring older person as someone who repeats the same stories, and parades the same opinions firmly rooted in the past, is not inaccurate but it is unjust, for it ascribes these features to calendar old age. People who have lived a long time, have lively minds and keep up with life, do not develop the habit of reiterating their past experiences. Those who do either never had the inner equipment which would have made them lively throughout their lives, or else the circumstances of their lives have narrowed. For if the present is restricted, uneventful and unchallenging, and the future is envisaged as inevitably worse still in every aspect, then it is natural enough to retreat more and more into the past. After all, in the past there was an active role to play, and the person was *somebody* then. But if the present is full and rewarding, then the future is taken care of as well; for if today is good and there is a lot to be done or thought about, these activities will carry on into the next day, the next year.

The view that old people are boring because they live in the past is an inversion of fact: they live in the past because their present is boring.

9
Attitudes Helpful to Older People

In the preceding chapters we have had a look at various aspects of how younger and older people interact and what difficulties they may encounter. Scattered through these chapters were remarks and reflections which indicated how problems might be avoided or remedied. In this chapter I want to draw together some thoughts into a more concentrated view of what attitudes and actions are likely to be of real benefit to the older, and indirectly to the younger, people involved.

The essential requirement for developing a helpful, positive attitude to older people is to get away from the stereotype view that calendar age, in itself, is important. On the contrary, it is the state of a person's health, the state of mind, the content of his or her life which are important. It is on these factors that the well-being of older people depends, and which dictate their needs.

Encouragement
What older people, as people of any age, thrive on is encouragement from those around them. Older people particularly need encouragement to retain, or to regain, self-confidence and self-reliance. This can be on a lofty level or on a trivial level. A reasonably fit adult of any age does not take kindly to being manipulated, and does not really thrive on being cared for and cosseted,

as a way of life. There is a great difference between an occasional spoiling or treat and a reduction of an older person to the position of a child, whose life is managed, guided, protected and shaped. Progressive loss of self-confidence is a real factor, and there is a real risk of producing it through over-protection (however lovingly motivated) from mental or physical exertion. Over-protection leads to over-dependence, and, perhaps paradoxically, to a 'grumbling insecurity' – a subconscious feeling that one is all right only so long as there is someone else to see to everything. We tend to trust too little the potential for capable self-management present in older people. And yet, most of us have come across cases where, for example, a widow formerly very much protected manages astonishingly well to look after her own affairs.

When I speak of that encouragement to live their own lives in their own way, which we should give to our elders, I do not advocate that we withdraw from them. To be really effective, encouragement has to have a background of affection, interest, respect, concern – and helpfulness. As with any person who means something to us, we should make it plain to our elders that should any help be needed at any time we are willing to give it. More than that, we should make it clear that we shall keep an eye open for any help being needed, and not just sit there waiting for our elders to come to us, cap in hand, or for an SOS message to be sent to us when a crisis has been reached.

Older people are not like children
This background of support, allied to freedom, provided by us for elders may make it appear that there is a parallel to the way we should treat our children. In fact, the parallel is only very superficial. Older people are not like children, who are without experience, and whose abilities and personalities are still to take shape. Of all the groups in society that of the elderly is the least

homogeneous. Older people are especially individual, because each one has lived a long time as that particular person, in his or her own right. It does not mean that they had reached some peak of development at the much-vaunted but largely ill-defined prime of their lives, and then started a descent backwards down a slope into childhood again. Peaks are many and different: the peak of having power over employees may have been reached by a man in his fifties or sixties; but his peak of understanding human nature may not come until he is in his seventies or eighties, at a time when he is a little removed from the actual turmoil of a working life. A woman's motherly gifts may have had their peak when her children were tiny, but her creative peak may only emerge when she takes up writing or painting in her later years. We may unwittingly cause older people to abdicate from trying to reach any peaks, or even to keep on a plateau, if we deprive them of having control over their own lives. Deprive is a harsh word to use, but it is possible to deprive someone of a chance of personal development (yes, even in old age this is perfectly possible), or of fulfilment, through an excess of love. Our elders do not need mothering. They need friendship and companionship to sustain and to embellish their lives – and it is these which we should try to give them. It may not always be that their own, particular style of life, or view of society, is what *we* think it ought to be. We feel entitled to resent it if other people suggest that we should change our lives or our views to conform with what they think is right. Our elders have just as much right to resent any interference from us. We do not even have the excuse of our greater experience, which may be valid when we deal with children but is not likely to impress our elders.

Expectations and realities
We tend to carry images in our minds of what people should be like, and feel cheated if they turn out to be different. We may

imagine that a grandmother should be a cosy little lady, who enjoys nothing more than surrounding her grandchildren with her loving and ever-present interest in every tiny detail of their lives. If the real-life grandmother happens to be a lady of strong intellect and of reserved personality, we may feel rather upset at times because she does not react to our children in the way our imaginary grandmother would. It is unrealistic and childish of us to feel upset like this, and unfair to the grandmother if we take out our disappointment on her in some way. It is not easy sometimes to give up an image, and to look really closely at what is valuable and life-enriching in people, as they are. As with other situations, if we try to put ourselves into the other's place we can hope to gain some insight and understanding. After all, most people like to think that they are loved, or valued for what they are, for their real selves, and not for some imaginary qualities. If this is true for ourselves, then it should be true for those we want to fit into an image. It would be more rewarding for everyone involved in that example if the reserved and intellectual grandmother were valued for what she can in reality give to her grandchildren, rather than regretting her failure to be a cosy dispenser of undemanding attention. Our expectations are likely to be fulfilled if they are based on a realistic view of those involved in a relationship and, practically speaking, it is easier to modify our expectations than to change people.

Attitude to health
Before we can encourage a positive and hopeful attitude to their health in older people, we have to develop it ourselves. We have been so brain-washed for years about ill-health and eventual invalidism being practically synonymous with old age, that it may take a real effort of thought and of will to evolve a more realistic attitude. As a basic principle we should never ascribe any deterioration in health to old age, and should guard our

elders from doing so. Older people may fall ill or have accidents, but they get over them, and their chances of recovery depend not on their calendar age, but on their constitution, the severity of the condition, or the effectiveness of the treatment given. An actual example points up what I mean: a lady in her forties broke a wrist and, unfortunately, had it badly set. The fracture healed, but the bones grew together so that the wrist remained slightly deformed. It took many months of physiotherapy to overcome the restricted mobility and the pain and even then the arm was not back to normal. The same lady had the bad luck to break the other wrist at the age of eighty-one. This time it was set properly; the bones knitted together and the plaster was taken off after the same interval of time as that allowed for youngsters with similar fractures. A few sessions of treatment in the physio-therapy department helped to strengthen and mobilise the arm and no further difficulties were experienced. It is an interesting example because it relates to the *same* person's experiences, forty years apart. It is important to realise how unimportant age is for two reasons. Firstly, it leads to therapeutic optimism, which enables us to believe that however old an ill person may be, the right treatment will produce a positive result, unless the disease is overwhelmingly severe, or the person is too frail. Secondly, it points up the importance of striving to remain, or to become, fit in old age, for the fitter the person the better the chance of recovering from medical or social adversity. If we keep these factors in mind we gain confidence in the health of our elders and then we can indeed help them to feel more confident about it.

Attitude to activities
As confidence should be the key to a positive attitude to the health of our elders, so expansionism should be the key to our attitude to their activities. It is a disservice we do our elders if, from the best motives, we tend to respond negatively to any

ideas or plans of theirs, because we feel it may be beyond their strength to carry them out. It may prove to be so; but is it not better to have a go at something, to try it out, and then to modify or give it up if need be, than to be discouraged from even trying? We should not discourage anyone who is reasonably fit from continuing doing something they enjoy, just because they are getting older and because we, in our conventional way of thinking about age, consider that it is no longer advisable for them for that reason. If it is beyond their strength, their own bodies and their commonsense will let them know soon enough. We should actively encourage and support the idea that, however old a person is, he or she is capable of having a go at something new. This idea should be supported by practical steps: the provision of opportunities and of facilities for expanding activities, for acquiring interests. We should generate a feeling that it is normal to be active and interested at any age. The case of the late James Chapman vividly illustrates that when opportunities are provided to do something new and interesting even an undoubtedly elderly man can respond with enthusiasm and delight to them. Mr Chapman was 103 years old when he said that more exciting and interesting things happened to him in the last three years of his life than in the first hundred: For him life began at a 100 – because people 'discovered' him then, realised how lively he was in spirit and fit in body, and offered him opportunities to do all sorts of things: driving a juggernaut lorry, going up in a hot-air balloon, flying a Tiger Moth, going down in a submarine. He had it in him to enjoy all these experiences to the full – and above all, he was prepared to have a go.

Attitude to interactions with other people
If our attitude is that humanity is fragmented into groups of people of particular ages, and they have nothing to give or to receive across these divisions, then indeed we create a 'generation

gap'. If we forget about age, and simply react to people, then the gap disappears. We often hear that older people are happier among their own contemporaries, that they do not understand the world of today, and are afraid of it. This may indeed be so, but possibly because nobody really takes the trouble to explain, or to communicate to them, what is happening around them. The key to our attitude about interactions with older people is very simple: they need not be treated as some sort of special group. They are neither mentally retarded, nor lacking in experience, nor are they visitors from another planet. If we can chat about our interests or ideas or mundane events to our friends, we can do so to our elders. If we have any affinity with them or fondness for them, so much the better. If we do not, but we still have contact with them, then it may take some effort perhaps, but this effort is likely to be repaid by the contact becoming more rewarding, or at any rate less dull.

If, for example, our elders tend to criticise and deplore modern youth, it may be that their experience of young people is very limited. It may be confined to television news items dealing with some loutish exploits, or offences against the law, by some young people. We cannot, under the circumstances, really blame them for their opinions. What we can do is to arrange for them to meet some young people in the flesh, who are worthwhile human beings, and who are unlikely to get into the news since they do not disrupt the peace. Our attitude in a case like this is all-important. We may think that old people always grumble about the present, and do not understand people of a different generation. Or we may recognise that an older person may have a wrong opinion because of ignorance, and we can try and alter that opinion. Older people are not as rigid and impervious to influence as we tend to imagine. We can be of real help to them by making them better informed. For instance, in the above example, meeting a few real young people may colour more accurately and more positively their view of a whole large sector of the world around them.

Our attitude to ourselves

Finally, and very importantly, what of our attitude to ourselves in our relationships with older people? If the older people are not disabled or extremely frail or ill, we should not regard ourselves as their keepers. If, as members of the 'managing generation', we stand in the middle between our children and our elders, we may be tempted to develop the same attitude towards both, and to see ourselves in the same role of mentor, guardian, 'manager' and guide *vis-à-vis* both. This, as we have seen earlier, is unlikely to benefit our elders, and it is not likely to benefit us. We are exposing ourselves to the risk of feeling put upon, of having to cope with everyone's problems and needs, and eventually of developing self-pity. If we see ourselves in the role of guardian angels, nurse-maids and business-managers, all rolled into one, then the effect on our elders will be a gradual erosion of their self-confidence and self-reliance, because we shall be depriving them of their *raison d'être* as adults.

An attitude of 'live and let live' will help our elders and it will help us too. It will free us from more responsibility or guilt than we can bear. To give a somewhat fanciful example: we should see ourselves as a safety net which gives confidence to the performer and saves him from injury should he fall, but which does not constrain or direct his efforts. We should not see ourselves as a puppet-master who jerks the strings this way or that.

Our attitudes often determine whether we in fact want to solve a particular problem or not. The man who phoned in to a radio programme, devoted to a discussion of difficulties facing those who care for elderly relatives, had a problem which was objectively very serious, but he also had a particular attitude to himself in his predicament. His problem was that he had not been able to get away from his home for years because of his invalid mother's needs. His attitude to his role in this situation was that of a martyr, for he resisted taking up any suggestions the panel proffered, such as having his mother admitted to hospital on a short-term basis, which could have helped him to have at least a brief respite. Why he had this attitude we cannot tell. Perhaps it earned him the approval of people. Perhaps he felt he was expiating some guilt. Perhaps it gave him a respectable excuse for opting out of other pursuits in life which he found burdensome. He seemed to be appealing for help, yet he did not really want to be helped. The aspect of this story which concerns me is this: how did his mother feel about being the cross which her son was so devotedly and unremittingly carrying? I wonder if he ever gave this any thought. A brief mental switching of situations may, at times, illuminate for us how our attitude to ourselves affects the fate of another person.

In all the endless variety of relationships between older and younger people, those attitudes are likely to have a positive effect which have as little as possible of self-importance, of self-righteousness or of self-pity in them, on either side. Liveliness of mind, warmth of heart, openness of approach, and generosity of response, are the qualities which, singly or in combination, make relationships flourish and so bring their own reward.

10
Opportunities for Involvement

Biological evidence and our own observation of elderly but active people suggest that a revision of our attitudes to ageing and to the elderly is necessary. If we accept this, then the next step is to have a look at some ways in which more positive attitudes can be translated into action.

The traditional ways of taking care of our elders, saving them from effort, sheltering them from the supposedly incomprehensible and alien world outside, these have little to offer to people who may be getting on in years but who are reasonably healthy and fit. We have to remember that these days people who retire at sixty or sixty-five may live perhaps twenty or thirty years in retirement. They do not become less capable of managing their lives the day after retirement than they were the day before. They may feel cut adrift for a while, and they do need help at this stage. They should be encouraged to remain active, not cosseted into putting up their feet in front of the fire, for the next few decades. Chances are that if they lapse into inactivity, they will not have any decades of good health ahead of them.

If we are to enrich and expand the lives of our elders, several important basic approaches will serve to illustrate the underlying principles.

Opportunities to give, as well as to receive

Just as in the physical world there is a tendency towards equilibrium, towards action and reaction, so in the emotional sphere there is a need to give as well as to receive.

Emotionally greedy, grasping, hoarding people are not healthy; they are trying to compensate for some lack in their inner lives. This lack may even be that of opportunities to give, or of a talent for giving. This possibility makes me feel that an older person who is dominating and demanding for attention, and on the face of it unlikely to be in need of giving, may, in fact, benefit from a chance to do so. The reason may be simple: in order to give, it is necessary to think of another person, and so some preoccupation with self will be diverted. It is far less simple to manage to introduce such a person to the idea and to the action of giving. It may require considerable ingenuity. Two ingredients are necessary: first, confidence that the person *has* something to give, and second, that a real need exists for that which the person is able to give. Depending on their personal qualities and abilities such older people could become involved in a great variety of useful and stimulating activities. To take a few examples: they could help set up a charity organisation or function, coach children in some skill or subject, drive people needing transport to hospital or to educational or recreational establishments, take up citizens' advice bureau work, or help in a library or in a school. Again depending on the particular person's make-up, the response may be positive either if a direct plea for help is made ('Mrs Jones, I'm ill in bed with flu – would you mind doing some shopping for me when you go out?'), or if the possibility of getting involved in giving some help is thoroughly and reasonably discussed beforehand. In either case there is need for tact, so that we do not appear to be foisting something unwanted onto an unwilling person.

At the other extreme there are older people all too willing to give, but who may be frustrated in this, through circumstances or through a lack of sensitivity on the part of people around them.

It may be argued that it is easy to involve your older relatives in some giving situation if you live in the same town or in the same house. Of course it is easier; but it is not impossible to think about this aspect of older people's lives, and to suggest or create opportunities, by post, or when on a visit, however great the geographic distance involved. Taking the saddest extreme, if we have a relative in an old people's home, we can involve her in helping us with knitting woollies for the children, or in making a rug, or in collecting some information from the newspapers which the children need for school, or in compiling a genealogy because younger members of the family may be interested to know something about their antecedents. This last point, incidentally, seems to exercise today's young people in North America. They are searching for roots, and grandparents or elderly relatives are often the link which can provide them with a sense of continuity. In this situation an older person is providing something intangible but very valuable for the stability and self-esteem of the younger ones.

There is something of immense value which older members of a family, grandparents especially, give – but this gift is not often enough acknowledged in so many words. Their existence, their experience, their personalities are this gift, because they extend and enrich the experience of life of the younger members simply by *being*, not by *doing* anything in particular for them. This gift may be taken quite for granted, by both the givers and the receivers, but it ought to be looked at from time to time, and its value voiced. To give just one example: a child or young person who is fortunate enough to have a grandparent who in calendar old age is vigorous, interested, and positive, has the inestimable boon of growing up with an optimistic view of the duration of active and enjoyable life. Only a rare child will have the insight to realise this, but the middle generation might reflect on it and mention it at some appropriate moment.

One of the most obvious and rewarding ways in which we may involve an older person in a giving situation is to ask for help in teaching or coaching a grandchild, or other small relative. On the whole, teaching is likely to be fraught with more difficulties than coaching. The reason is, I think, that a child finds it difficult to reconcile the domestic front, and the personages involved in it, with a 'school' situation. Children are probably very different people at home and at school, and this is quite natural. We all have our family persona, our professional one, our social one, and so on. Adults have very clear personas in children's minds, and an especially close relationship with a grandparent, for example, may be a real hindrance to the success of the grandparent's teaching a more formal subject to the grandchild. It is not so if, instead of teaching something from scratch, a grandparent is involved in supervising, or coaching, or 'helping' with an activity or subject taught by somebody else. This activity can be most rewarding for both sides. The child can learn from the experienced adult how to tackle the work – and the adult will see progress being made thanks to his or her efforts. Some grandparents are especially successful when they take up the attitude that they will learn together about the particular subject which their grandchildren find boring or difficult. This often involves the grandparent in tackling something new, and that is an added refreshment. To give an actual example: a grandmother, who is a music-lover but not a musician, found a great deal of interest in helping a grandchild on a let's learn-it-together basis with the theory of music syllabus required for a higher grade music examination. This type of activity is co-operative and it forges a bond between the particular people involved, which has far more meaning than any formal once-a-week visits to Granny could ever achieve. No such lasting and valuable links can be formed by giving material presents. A child is not often taken in by being showered with gifts and is quick to sense when an adult has no real interest in the child and no wish to devote time or thought to him.

There are innumerable things that grandparents and grand-children can do together, and one of the most important advantages that grandparents have, compared with parents, is the availability of time. The idea that grandparents are the people who tell the children about the past is valid. They are the transmitters of traditions and of family lore, and the givers of a sense of continuity. But present-day grandparents are far too little stretched, if the only thing expected of them is to delve into the past. They can be involved in much more active exploration and adventure with their grandchildren to great mutual benefit. They can take the grandchildren to museums, to exhibitions, plays, sporting events, on fishing trips, and even, if means permit, on really exciting travels. This way the world really expands for both of them; the parents also benefit, because their children grow up with a much enriched view of life. The parents have to do one thing for themselves, though: to have confidence in the grandparents, and to trust the children to them without emotional strings attached. The relationship between the grandparents and the grandchildren has to be allowed to develop directly, and not filtered through the parents' mental or emotional attitudes. A gentle reminder to thank Grandpa for a marvellous day's fishing, or a hint that a grandchild at the end of a long day may be crotchety from sheer tiredness, is as far as one need to go in steering the interaction between the two generations.

On the whole, children form good relationships with adults, either because they live in a family where there is affection and respect among its members and so they follow this natural path in their own lives; or they form a good relationship with some particular adult, as a refuge from less satisfactory relationships with, or among, other members of the family. In either case all they need basically is a positive and welcoming response from the adult. Children do not need directives about how to manage the relationship. Nor, of course, do the grandparents need detailed instructions on how to treat their grandchildren when the parents are not there. The sort of mother who leaves a perfectly fit child in the care of a perfectly able and sensible grandmother for a few days, and writes down several pages of detailed instructions about eating, going to bed, washing, etc., insults the adult and deprives the child of a chance of tasting a different way of life.

Even when a grandparent is fortunate enough to have the means for a really exciting adventure with the grandchildren it can be spoiled by the parents' attitude. A magnificent experience which a grandmother invited her two young granddaughters to share with her, was a tour by air from London to Leningrad, then to legendary places like Samarkand, to Moscow, and back to London. This was in early summer, but the heat in the Central Asian desert was such that the temperature was over 120°F in the shade; the flights were long; the sightseeing arduous. But for all of them this was a part of a most exciting adventure, and a unique experience shared. And yet it could have been spoiled by a lack of confidence on the parents' part, because it would have made the grandmother uneasy about the responsibility of taking the girls on such a long and strenuous journey. It would also have undermined her self-confidence in her own state of health and in her strength. As it was, they were kissed goodbye at the airport with no 'words of wisdom' to haunt them on their marvellous journey.

The above example is real, and it illustrates another point: the generation gap does not come about through some law of nature. When there is an interest in common, or an activity or an adventure shared, then there are strong and living bonds between the generations, not gaps. The gaps are there when age, as such, is seen as something in the forefront rather than in the background of human interactions, as though birth-dates rather than people matter in their own right. Parents tend to create a gap between the grandparents and the grandchildren if they 'hover': if they feel, or, worse still, express anxiety that Grandma or Grandpa will find it too much to have a grandchild to stay, or to take on an outing. If it turns out that it was too much, for some reason, then the parents can act accordingly next time. But chances are that it has not been too much, it may even not have been enough – and so there was no need to have had any doubts about the grandparent's endurance. An interest or a responsibility tends to generate energy in most people, and makes them feel more alive and capable. So grandchildren left on their own with grand-parents probably see a far more active and lively aspect of them than do the parents. A man of eighty who tended to doze off in his chair a good deal of the time was quite happy to mark an occasion by taking his eighteen-year-old granddaughter out to dinner, and spending a delightful and memorable evening with her. The interdependence of body and mind is a very real factor which accounts for the way a mental or emotional stimulus can summon up our physical resources.

Let us now take a look at the particular circumstance of living in one household with our elders. Such an arrangement both provides additional opportunities for a give-and-take life-style, and creates some difficulties. Most of the difficulties arise from a reluctance, or an omission, to discuss matters thoroughly and sensibly, at an early stage of sharing life in the same household. The healthiest way to make such a household run well and benefit all its members is to share its comforts *and* its duties and responsibilities. The older person should neither be smothered in a cocoon of loving care, nor put upon by a family which is quite unwilling to make any adjustments. All members of the family should be able to lead a normal life. The management generation, particularly the female member of it, should not set off on a spiral of ever-increasing duties and chores, and become unable to let go of any of them. That is not good management. A frazzled person at the centre of a household is no joy to anyone. It is far wiser to sort out with all the members of the household which areas should be looked after by whom, and then to let each member get on with their job, without interference or anxious supervision. If the sphere of influence is chosen realistically and suitably at the start, then there should not be any worry as to whether the older person can or cannot cope with his task. If Grandfather or Great-aunt is a gardener, then let them garden – and enjoy the benefit of it physically, psychologically and aesthetically. If Grandma is musical, then let her supervise the children's piano practice; if she is a wonderful cook, let her cook the special dishes for your dinner parties. Better still, encourage *her* to give her own dinner parties.

In any household there are possibilities of every member contributing something useful and valuable. The type of person who makes it impossible for anyone else to help, or to take some chores off her hands, is not a marvellous housewife. She is either a martyr who needs to feel put upon, or she craves power to the extent that she must hold the threads of all the household's activities. Offers of help, like signs of affection, should be welcomed – not brushed aside. If Grandma offers to cook the evening meal a couple of times a week, then do agree. Take this chance to do a course, or go out to the theatre, or visit friends, or take a part-time job. In this way Grandma will be contributing to the family, you will have time for yourself, and the family will have a change from your cooking.

The essence of harmonious living in a two- or three-generation family is integration. This is naturally easiest if the people involved are on the same 'wave-length' personally and culturally – then there is no problem at all. But even in less fortunate circumstances it is possible to enhance those aspects which are positive, and put the negative ones into perspective. A sharing of activities and spheres of influence helps integration; it helps to break down the 'us' and 'them' atmosphere which can develop if some members become too passive and others have an unfair load of duties to carry. Another thing which is essential for successful integration is the feeling of freedom, which all the members should have, to do some things together with the others and some things separately from them. Integration presupposes tolerance of people in their own right, and a willingness to compromise. To put it simply: in a harmonious household each member will feel that without any of the others life would be less good. Such a situation is not an impossibility. To create it a certain amount of thinking about it initially, and of working at it subsequently, are necessary, since only very few people manage by instinct to do all the right things all the time.

Paradoxically, a harmonious household may inhibit older persons from seeking wider contacts and interests outside. If we have their well-being at heart, then we should encourage them to be active outside the family, to interact with other people, to enhance their feeling of identity as individuals apart from the corporate membership of the family. It may well be the stuff of life for an older person to be John's mother or Jane's grandmother, but it is refreshing from time to time for her to be just Mrs Smith to somebody who does not necessarily even know about the existence of either John or Jane.

Conclusion

We are the 'older members of the family' of tomorrow, and if we think about this from time to time, it should be easier for us to create and maintain as positive and life-enhancing a relationship as possible with our elders. After all, we need only think of how *we* would like to be situated when *we* are the older people within a family group. On our way to that position we would benefit from questioning many stereotypes connected with ageing, in its physical, mental and social aspects. In the course of such rethinking we should gain a good deal of insight into the reality, rather than the stereotype, of getting older in our day and age. If we now help our elders to forget their age and to participate fully in the life around them, then we are likely to have the same boon from our younger relatives, when we in our turn come to be the senior generation. Nothing impresses more or teaches better than example. The management generation, by showing real concern for the well-being of their elders, at the same time educate their juniors to have a positive and a more realistic view of ageing. In these circumstances the middle generation gain from both sides. Their elders, through being more active and expansionist, are fitter, more alert, and less 'difficult' people than they might otherwise be. Their juniors are imbued with a view of older people which will ensure a better deal for the middle generation in their later years. In this way true concern for others and self-interest will merge. This should spur us towards expansionism and integration as our goals for our elders today and for ourselves tomorrow!

PART IV
Attitudes to Older People Within the Community

11

The Well-being of Older People Within a Community

Although the family may be regarded as a community, in this chapter I intend to project the discussion onto a wider screen, and to take a look particularly at groups where older people are segregated.

The attitudes of the management generation who care for elderly people in segregated groups have a direct bearing on how these older people live. These groups may be found in hospital wards, old people's homes, old people's clubs, and day centres. Some of these establishments may be splendidly, imaginatively and humanely run, but some are not. Although lack of finance, and lack of facilities or of staff may be responsible for various shortcomings, the main responsibility for the climate of an establishment rests with the people who are involved.

Possible reasons for negative attitudes
It may be that our sensibilities are too tender for us to be confronted with a human being who is ill, neglected, abandoned or depressed, and we shrink from admitting to ourselves that inside this human being is a *person*. We can only cope with this situation by pretending to ourselves that we are faced with someone different from us: a pet, a child, a cross-to-be-borne, or a patient. If that is how we function, basically we have not the

inner strength to be in a caring profession or a caring situation, and we shall fail those in our charge, fail them fundamentally and unpardonably. It is in no way their fault that we cannot really cope with other people's needs or sufferings.

If we genuinely believe that a neat, tidy, orderly establishment is good for all those within it, we shall put these priorities first. If we do, it is very much easier to function if we look no deeper than the surface of the people in our care. If we do look deeper we may find all sorts of untidy individualisms which will be difficult to marshall into a homogeneous neatness. It may be that we like power, and we may find it uncomfortable that people who come under our care happen to have had a long life and have become ever more individual. It is easier to exert power, if we either build ourselves up to be bigger than most, or if we diminish those we have to deal with. The latter is again easier to achieve if we do not look too closely to see whether there is a person inside those who are in our power. It may be that we simply do not give much thought to people we care for pro-fessionally and so treat them, without meaning any harm, in ways which may upset them.

Many other reasons may account for our inability or unwilling-ness to recognise the incontrovertible fact that in every human being there is a person, at all ages and at all moments of life. It is not important in the present context to delve into these various reasons, but it is important to see what this non-recognition of persona means to older people.

Some consequences of failing to recognise a person within a human being
Any attitude which robs a person of human identity, of persona, is bad. From such attitudes flows behaviour towards people which may be unkind, hurting, diminishing, humiliating, or depriving.

It may be all right for our dentist to think of us as 'that

troublesome upper left canine', or for our hairdresser to recognise us as someone who is 'thin on top but with plenty to cut behind the ears'. These people see us infrequently, and attend to our specific needs at specific times. But in a hospital ward we should not be 'the hernia by the window', or 'the fracture with a bad cough'. If we are, then there is something seriously wrong with the way the ward is run. The difference is that the staff on the ward come into much closer contact and a more prolonged contact with us, than does the dentist or the hairdresser. In a closer interaction, to rob patients of persona is to diminish them. Even worse is this effect in a home for old people, for staff here can make all the difference to the quality of life of the residents. I do not know the motive which prompted a staff member of a home to say to an 85-year-old resident who had bought herself a new coat: 'Isn't it a bit of a waste at your age?' I assume it was not said because the younger woman regarded the older one as her bitterest enemy. The fact remains that she conjured up the spectre of death in front of another human being, and did not for a moment think of her as a person who may fear death.

Segregated groups, be they patients in a ward or residents in a home, who are treated like senile children, who are addressed by their first names without being invited to do so, who are given odd garments – odd stockings even – to wear, who are sat on chairs, without undergarments because of possible incontinence – all these unfortunate people have suffered from this one thing, the fundamental refusal, on the part of those who care for them, to see them as persons. The euphemism of 'care' under these circumstances is nauseating, for such treatment has nothing to do with caring, but only with the containment of people within four walls, as refuse may be contained in a bin. A situation as bad as this does not arise as an inevitable result of putting together certain ingredients. The ingredients of old people who may be ill or may have no other home, and younger people who have to look after them, possibly in unsatisfactory or inadequate physical surroundings, can come together and, given a different attitude, can result in a decent regard for the older *person*.

Some unfortunate ways of treating older people

When our obsession with calendar age is allied to a stereotyped view that 'old' equals 'like a child' (and then not a very bright child, as like as not), we come to treat older people in all sorts of unfortunate ways. Patronising forms of address, calling older women 'dear' or men 'dad'; making polite but inane remarks to an older person present, before getting down to 'proper talking' with a younger one, although the former may be by far the more interesting human being of the two; not bothering to discuss with older people matters affecting them, or to ask their views; talking about them to a third party, in their presence, as though they either cannot hear or cannot understand what is being said; responding to any remark which an older person may make about some ache or pain, by saying 'It's just age' or 'What can you expect? You are not getting any younger.' These are some of the unfortunate things we do.

The generation gap between young staff and old patients or residents is, as in any other context, the result of a failure in communication, which in itself results from a failure to think about the other person. Perhaps a trivial but actual example will serve to illustrate this. A young nurse, who noticed during a group physiotherapy session that an elderly woman patient seemed anxious, called out to her across the room 'Oh, Mrs X, do you want to go to the loo?' A helpful remark from an observant nurse, you might think. Not so, since the form in which it was put upset the patient. She had not been brought up in the freer and more 'natural' atmosphere now prevailing in our society, and to her a stark query about the loo was unacceptable, especially as it was shouted across the room for all to hear.

Institutionalised human beings

The attitude which assumes that older people are best looked after by being spoon-fed, and discouraged from any self-help or decision-making, produces 'institutionalised human beings'. If it were discovered that, let us say, a contaminant in the water supply to a district produced lethargy, inertia, physical and mental decline, depression, apathy, and eventually physical breakdown and mental confusion among the elderly residents, drastic measures would be swiftly taken to trace the source of the contaminant, and to purify the water supply. The symptoms mentioned above do occur among institutionalised elderly people, and the 'contaminant' causing these symptoms is the mental attitude of those persons who decide what is done, or is not done, in the old people's home. If life is deprived of purpose, then there is nothing left for an older person to do but to give up. Some do it gradually, some precipitately. The transposition from one's own style of life, from privacy, from companionship of choice, from being a distinct person, to a situation of crowded loneliness and rigid, empty routine is traumatic in itself. Existence under such conditions saps the essence of being a person in one's own right. Physical inactivity impairs health; lack of stimulation, of interests, of impressions, leads to mental torpor; lack of emotional outlets leads to withdrawal, to depression, to misery. People in these conditions do have food and shelter, but their life is turned into mere existence. Attitudes of the powers-that-be which produce such conditions are as harmful to the elderly as are bacteria or viruses. That is a very black picture of living in an old people's home, and one hopes that institutions which are dominated by such attitudes are becoming more and more rare. Even so, it is necessary to realise that less dramatic but still undesirable ill-effects may result from less drastically unenlightened views among those responsible for the style of life in institutions, and impair the well-being of the older people.

Sops instead of opportunities

Our stereotype of an elderly person as someone who is unable to manage much, who is less able or capable than a younger person, also leads us to assume that the last thing fit older people need or want is to be stretched, physically and mentally. So we end up with such time-wasting and totally unstretching pursuits as bingo in old people's clubs. The provision of such an amenity is based on an assumption, which ignores that the potential for doing new, interesting and meaningful things is possessed by as many elderly people blessed with sufficient intelligence, as by younger people equally blessed. As long as we refuse to recognise that older people are people who do not become mental defectives at the stroke of age sixty-five, so long shall we offer them time-wasting sops, instead of opportunities for using their time to some purpose. As in other contexts, expectations tend to fulfil themselves, and the more we expect of people, the more they prove to be capable of extending themselves.

Attitudes of society to older people

Projecting our discussion onto a still wider screen, let us consider what too often happens when society bestirs itself on behalf of its older members.

(a) *Health care.* The far too prevalent view taken of 'senior citizens' is that of human wreckage or of a vast reservoir of ill-health, disability, apathy, poverty and a sort of universal mindlessness, which has no need of any life-enhancement. This view of old age is, fortunately, less often projected by the media now than it was in the past. But the various surveys and statistical studies, which are conducted to determine what are likely to be the needs of society in the decades to come for the care of the elderly, still concentrate too much on custodial care for the incapable and too little on supportive measures for the fit. People engaged in constructing models for future requirements seem to feel intuitively that the most sensible way to use resources for the elderly would be to allocate generously to preventative aspects of health care and social welfare, to positive health measures. Yet it is a strange thing that they cannot construct a suitable model which would take into account the effects of such measures! So the traditional forecasts go on, and we have more predictions of the numbers of geriatric beds, which will be required, and of the astronomical costs of it all. If medical thinking remains static, and the needs of today are projected a decade ahead, and if one takes into account the rising numbers of people who survive into old age, then there is little doubt that all these extra beds will indeed be filled. When one realises that the number of people aged sixty or over in this country today is of the order of nine million, it becomes obvious that it is high time for some fresh thinking to be done now. Retired people have a personal right to a full and active life, and provision of opportunities for such a life is a sound national investment. Geriatric beds, and staff to run geriatric wards, are very, very expensive items in looking after older people. Better pensions, better opportunities for free-lance work, better housing, better educational and recreational facilities, free transport, subsidised holidays, adequately paid domestic help, decent financial aid to relatives who have to look after elderly people – measures like these would allow older people to live with dignity and in better health and spirits. In terms of cash and of manpower such provisions may well cost less than ever-increasing custodial care.

Global costing of such alternatives would be a very interesting exercise. Where this has been done it has revealed some rather surprising situations. For example, it has been found in France that it costs the community less to pay for an elderly patient's off-season holiday on the Riviera in a good hotel, than it costs to keep such a long-stay patient in hospital, for the same period of time. Not only does the patient benefit from a change, but the community actually saves money. It has been speculated that it might be cheaper to send older people, who are prone to respiratory troubles during the winter, on a two or three months' holiday in Spain, rather than have them hospitalised here during that period. It is unfortunate that global costing is so rarely done, or at least so rarely made available to the public. Costs are habitually pronounced to be too high – but we are not told what they are being compared to, or what the alternatives cost. It is rather like soap powder advertisements which claim that a particular powder 'washes whiter'. Whiter than what? We tend to be far too meek about this, we do not press for details, for a balance sheet as it were.

(b) *Retirement.* If the problem of positive health care for older people is one in need of urgent constructive thinking, so of course is the related problem of compulsory retirement. Society cannot go on accumulating more and more people who are compulsorily retired at sixty or sixty-five and who then live in boredom, idleness and in financial straits for twenty or thirty years. They are neither productive nor affluent enough to be real consumers; they claim supplementary benefits, welfare and other hand-outs. The glib talk of retiring people even earlier is all very well, but what shall we do with them, or for that matter, what will they do with themselves for perhaps a quarter of a century or more? We cannot be thinking that the sheer frustration and boredom of too early retirement will pop them into geriatric beds for a spell, and then smartly kill them off, thus solving the problem of a population top-heavy with retired workers. This problem has to be faced, let alone solved, and we have to make an early start doing it.

Continuing education throughout adulthood, training and retraining for changing jobs and professions, these are the most likely means of producing worthwhile alternatives to the present pattern of a period of education, followed by a period of work which ends in compulsory retirement. Such a pattern is too rigid, and it provides no openings for people in occupations other than the one for which they initially trained. Older people are likely to have qualities which would fit them very well for occupations which provide a service rather than produce goods: insight into human nature, experience of life, greater tolerance, better judgement. People in middle life, engaged in a productive industry, who are given the opportunity for training and offered the possibility of a career structure in a 'service' field, may well find a new vitality and continue to be productive in another sense.

Much more flexible ideas about employment will have to be used, and much more flexible conditions of employment will have to be worked out. Part-time work, longer annual holidays, secondments and exchanges, may all help to refresh older workers without resorting to the guillotine of abrupt and total retirement at a fixed age. Retirement should be a matter of choice, and should be dictated by the suitability or otherwise of the man for the job and the job for the man. In former times retirement for a manual worker was a release from often unbearable conditions. Men in the learned professions, in business, in law, in creative work, are not so rigidly held to a compulsory retirement age and they benefit from this. In compulsory retirement policies the factor of paramount importance is age – not the quality or the qualities of the person, nor the global benefit or otherwise to society. These are social issues and therefore political issues.

They require honest thinking by the best brains, and they require an interested involvement of all sections of society and of all political parties. Raising of the pensions by a few pounds by one government, or cutting back on welfare services by another, does not constitute a policy about retirement, about continuing education, about health or social welfare, neither for those who are already elderly, nor for those who will become elderly in the next decade or two.

Among the elderly of this country there must be plenty of talent, experience and imagination in many fields – in politics, law, economics, and industry – which could be used effectively to reform the whole concept of training, education and work. Retired people have the advantage of being free from daily concerns with specific work problems, and so can stand back and take a wider view of the need for change. After all, their experience will have covered *all* the stages – of training, work *and* retirement – and they can evaluate the merits or otherwise of each, and of their relationship to one another. The argument that older people may be out of touch with modern developments is not really relevant. From all sides we hear of the sad state of our economy, of our society, of our political life. So there is little justification for clinging to our modernity, and some basic clear thinking, ancient or modern, is what we need most.

(c) *Social welfare.* In providing social welfare for the elderly we are largely preoccupied with providing services for those who are unable to lead a wholly independent life. This is right and necessary, but it is not enough. From all that I have said before it will be clear that I regret the lack of expansionist facilities and opportunities for older people. These should be as integral a part of social welfare provision as meals-on-wheels or home helps. Too much emphasis is given to the elderly as recipients and not nearly enough as contributors and doers. It is again a question of attitudes and of preconceived ideas. A telling comment on existing welfare services comes from newly retired people. When asked why they do not attend a club or a day centre for older people, they often reply that *they* are not old, and 'going to those places with all those old people will make me old'. That is not always a fair view. Many of the clubs and centres are in fact excellent, and provide plenty of interesting activities and opportunities for members to run their own affairs. But the general image is of a place full of passive, segregated old people filling in time with undemanding and unstimulating pursuits.

The social welfare needed by reasonably fit, reasonably vigorous people of retirement age is of a different sort. They need opportunities for extending their knowledge, their involvement and their usefulness. None of these are likely to be provided if we cling to the view that older people are unable to learn new things, and are unable to form new relationships. (The fallacy of this view is discussed at the end of this chapter.) It is time to recognise that indeed they can do both, given the chance and the encouragement.

There is a good deal to reflect upon in a situation where transport is laid on for older people to attend a club where they play bingo, but no transport is available to take them to Further Education classes. A similar attitude on our part to the educational needs of children would lead us to provide, for children of all ages and all mental abilities, nothing but play-groups. This is patently absurd. It is also absurd to lump together all elderly people of a district, and provide facilities based on the lowest common level of interests, abilities and fitness.

(d) *Does mental decline inevitably come with age?* The idea that older people cannot learn new things has been unfortunately much supported by the often-quoted story that our brains all lose millions of cells every day, once we are 'past our prime'. But the notion of massive and universal brain cell loss is in point of fact based on extremely flimsy evidence. The experimental findings were published in 1919, and referred to a very small number of human brains, preserved in an anatomy museum. This means that the brains had been treated chemically, and their cellular structure was much altered by the treatment. Nothing was known to the experimenter about the medical or personal history of the people whose preserved brains he had examined. The technical procedure of such experiments, in which the cells are counted, of necessity deals with only a minute piece of the whole brain. Using proper scientific criteria, this study warranted *no conclusions whatever* regarding the fate of brain cells with increasing age. Experiments to study the effects of ageing are, by their very nature, long-term, and counting cells in a tissue is extremely tedious. It is not surprising, therefore, that there have not been sufficient attempts to verify in a scientifically reliable manner the conclusions reached in 1919. Various workers, at different times, have counted brain cells in animal and in human brains, but always the numbers of subjects studied were quite inadequate. The findings of these workers provided insufficient evidence for concluding that the changes observed were due to age differences alone. And yet just such conclusions were confidently published! What is worse, these conclusions have been dogmatically quoted in scientific, in medical and in lay circles for decades, and in the process have acquired the character of fact.

A recent study on mouse brains was much more carefully designed and carried out. It showed that in these brains there was no loss of cells with increasing age. It may be that some substances within the cells do, in fact, change with age, but this is something which has yet to be experimentally demonstrated. Certainly, on present evidence, we must not accept that people become less able mentally because, as they grow older, their brains suffer a massive loss of cells.

There is evidence that older people who fail to learn new tasks as quickly as younger people do, are in a state of subconscious anxiety, produced by their expectation of failure. This lack of confidence in success is the result of years of brain-washing, of repeatedly hearing that it is more difficult to learn anything as you grow older. In fact, motivation, interest and encouragement are far greater spurs to successful learning than calendar young age. After all, there are thousands of young children and young people who learn very poorly indeed, if *their* motivation and interest are low, and encouragement is lacking.

These points, and the experience one has that people old in years can continue in mental vigour all their lives (and this is true for ordinary people as well as for many famous ones), gives one confidence that inevitable mental decline with advancing years is a myth.

12

The Quality of Life in Our Later Years

In the last chapter I discussed some attitudes which are likely to affect negatively the well-being of older people. I shall not now list a selection of attitudes which are the opposite of those described before, but rather I shall try to sketch in a way of looking at older people as an integral part of the community, be it a family, a local area, or the population of a country.

Dual aspects
There are several sets of two strands, as it were, involved in the problem of achieving a worthwhile quality of life for people in their later years. There is first the short-term concern for those who are already elderly now, and the long-term concern for the way the young of today will grow older. The answers to the former lie in enlightened thinking about priorities and in the provision of opportunities and of choices. The answers to the latter lie in enlightened education. Both need liberation from rigid and false views of ageing.

Another set of two strands involves motives. Action may, and should, spring from a deep human concern for the well-being of older people, and also from self-interest. If we work for improvements in the quality of life for others now, we are obviously building our own future on a solid foundation.

Yet another set of two strands concerns the responsibility of the individual for his own range of activities and interests, and the responsibility of the community for providing the means and opportunities for expanding the individual's horizons.

There are always two strands in the type of needs that have to be met: the needs of the physically, mentally or socially disadvantaged older people, and the needs of the more fortunate, the physically and mentally fit, older people, The confusion which often arises because 'the needs of the elderly' are lumped together, without a clear distinction being made between these two strands, has perpetuated a stereotyped view that *all* older people *inevitably* need *care*. They all need *thought*: some need care, and others need opportunities for developing their own resources and using them.

In contrast, we suffer from an over-rigid division of humanity, in all manner of contexts, into 'people' and 'old people'. We regard them as being in some mysterious way quite different in their needs, abilities, qualities and even emotions. Our emphasis on calendar age enhances this rigidity, and colours our attitudes. There is a very good reason why we really have to stop and rethink our views on how the quality of life may be improved for older people: their number in our society is already far greater than would constitute a 'minority', and this number is steadily rising. The impact of this situation on our institutions and social structures will be very strong. The impact would already be stronger than it is at present, if inertia and the habit of sweeping difficult problems under the carpet were not as strong as they are. It is no longer a question of only a few retired people in any given community living out a few years; it is a question of some nine million persons who are the retired and the elderly in this country now. These people have a right to expect to be fit, active and useful for many years after the age of compulsory retirement. If these expectations are to be fulfilled, then two fundamental changes seem to be necessary: the individual must stop believing that *age*, of itself, is responsible for automatic and inevitable decline; and society must stop regarding older people as a separate species.

The freelancing population

There is much searching for an acceptable way of referring to older people, and none of the terms used seems to have much appeal. 'Old people', 'senior citizens', 'pensioners' or 'old age pensioners' all seem to isolate a group within the community, and either to brand them as 'has beens' or to mock their lack of esteem by calling them 'senior'. With the proportion of the productive members of the population to the unproductive ones (which includes children and young people continuing their education, as well as the retired) steadily diminishing, it seems absurd that perhaps a fifth of the country's population are reduced to being 'pensioners'. If the productive members constitute the 'working population', then we should strive to make older people members of the 'freelancing population'. This concept would reflect more correctly their large numbers; it would not isolate them, but would unite them with all those members of the general population, who are not rigidly slotted into some full-time employment; it would also recognise the fact that older people have skills and experience and talents which they may employ – when and as they wish – on a freelance basis.

It may be argued that the *way* we refer to older people is not of particular importance, but I believe that it is important, because it brings our ideas into a sharper focus. If we talk about 'old people' we are likely to think that meals-on-wheels or geriatric beds are top priority. If we talk about the 'freelancing population', we are likely to realise that they have something of value to contribute and that their needs are no different from those of people in the mainstream of life. A very different set of criteria about the quality of their life thus emerges.

If society accepts that a large, and growing, section of its population will move from being part of the working population to being part of the freelancing population, many economic and social adjustments will need to be made. Important problems will need to be examined with open minds. The question of compulsory retirement age is one of these problems and the merits of gradual phasing out of a particular job is another. The eventual abolition of the earnings rule will indeed be a progressive step, for it will remove a deterrent which makes people reluctant to take a useful job and so to remain active. The fact of remaining active is the particularly important aspect in this situation, even more so than the extra money earned, and all that it can provide.

There is so much talk at present about our society crumbling under its load of difficulties and heading for disintegration, that it might be the right moment to devote some constructive thinking to the fundamental changes in the pattern of our population and how to get the best out of these changes. The vast resources of skills and experience available should not be allowed to become redundant from one day to the next at age sixty-five. If it is argued that promotions in jobs will be blocked by those who do not elect to retire, then career structures of employment should be revised. There may be quite effective ways of allowing people to retrain: or to step sideways into other areas of activity, within their place of work. For example, a technical man may, with increasing experience of life and a growing insight into human problems, become more valuable in the personnel than in the technical department of his firm.

One of the clichés of our time is that we are a 'work-oriented' society. So we are, and so we shall remain, presumably for a long time to come. If work is so important, then it is all the more vital to consider very carefully how to arrange our working lives in a way that would preserve, and enhance, the *quality* of our lives. For this the basic need is flexibility. We need to break out of the rigid cage of ideas and attitudes forged in the days of the Industrial Revolution, and of its aftermath of exploitation on the one hand, and of fighting for basic rights on the other. Flexibility is needed at all levels, of employers, as well as employees, of administrators as well as trade unionists. They need to think ten or twenty years ahead; they need to see how greatly the real problems facing them are changing.

Economic aspects

The economics of many aspects of life in our society will also need rethinking. Here it is not so much flexibility which is of primary importance as a careful balancing of the cost of alternative situations. We are far too often told that a given change or improvement will cost too much. Too much compared with what? It almost seems as if a sort of vacuum represents the status quo – a vacuum which costs nothing to maintain. But this is patently nonsense. If schools are bad, for example, then the community has to spend money on dealing with children who get into trouble and become involved with probation officers, or child psychologists. The activities of such people cost money. Do we ever see a 'balance sheet' in which the costs of providing better schools are compared with the savings on all the 'rescue' services or law-enforcement personnel who have to be involved – and paid for – now because many existing schools can provide neither a stimulating education nor environment?

Similarly, it will cost money to provide facilities of further education, of retraining, or of qualifying in a new skill, for the benefit of those who have retired from 'productive employment'. But if these able, and above all motivated, people use such facilities, and acquire new skills, they may form a reserve force for some of those services which are perpetually short of staff.

If the personnel in the field of social services, for instance, were reinforced by such retired people, a good deal of difficulty could be avoided by having enough people to tackle problems as they arise, instead of letting them pile up and so become less and less readily soluble.

A network of day centres, which exists already and which deserves to be expanded, provides opportunities to use actively the resources of the older people themselves. In many centres active participation and decision-making are encouraged in organising and in running various activities. Wherever this happens, enthusiasm is generated because the talents, the interests and the abilities of the participants are engaged. Enthusiasm is catching – it promotes vitality and it leads to success.

In some areas day centres could, perhaps, develop an employment bureau service as well, to provide an informal 'bridge' between the local employers and those older people who wish to do some paid work. Work centres and workshops for the retired contribute splendidly to the well-being of those older people who need both some extra earnings and companionship. They also fill a real industrial need; the work which is obtained from industry really needs doing, it is not a hand-out to keep some oldsters occupied! The more work centres and workshops show that older people are capable of doing a good job and doing it reliably and punctually, the more accustomed employers will become to the idea that there is a reservoir, a work force, which they can call upon, particularly if they need special skills, experience, and motivation.

The cost of providing flexible part-time employment, and of opportunities for voluntary work need to be balanced—against the cost to the community of growing numbers of unoccupied, bored and unproductive older people. They represent far too great a proportion of the country's human resources either to be wasted or to be nursed at a prodigious cost to the country.

The contribution to the economy which older people could make as consumers clearly depends on their having adequate financial resources. Since something like 15 per cent of the total population is aged sixty or over, their contribution could indeed be significant.

Education

As the solution to most problems an individual may face lies fundamentally in clear thinking, so the solution to most social problems lies fundamentally in education. Our system of education of young people tends to teach them about the world they live in, but not very much about either living or attitudes. It is never too early to teach children the *biological possibility* of remaining vigorous and capable even in old age. If they grasp this, then they can begin to build a positive attitude to their own, still remote but nonetheless real, fate as older adults, and they can also develop a more realistically thoughtful and encouraging attitude to those who are old already. Many young people do have the wish to help older people; they can do this so much better if they realise that there are many ways of helping. It may be wheeling a handicapped old lady out for a walk, or it may be encouraging grandfather to take up cycling again and riding with him just for the sheer enjoyment of it!

To live well and to age well, young people, children even, should be encouraged to look at life as a continuum, during the whole of which people can go on being interested and interesting, able and capable, gifted, and growing in wisdom and in experience, independently of their calendar age. It is difficult to project this idea in the face of the cliché that these days the world is changing so fast that *older people* cannot keep up with it. What world? The world of science and technology has, of course, changed extraordinarily quickly over the last century or so. But can *younger people* – all of them – keep up with these technological and scientific changes? Nobody, young or old, who is not a trained expert can possibly 'keep up' with such changes. The overwhelming majority of people in the world know little, and understand less, about either science or technology. They use the end products of scientific discovery and of technological progress, but these could just as well be produced by black magic, as by rational means, as far as their understanding of the processes involved is concerned. Some of them may be employed in jobs dealing with the production of tin cans, or of motor cars or vaccines – within that narrow scope of required understanding anyone, of *any age*, with sufficient training, can surely keep abreast of progress. So it is absolutely unnecessary to stigmatise an older person as some type of moron who cannot keep up with changes.

The world of human emotions, of human relations, which involves understanding, wisdom, judgement, a sense of proportion and of humour, does not basically change very fast, if at all. Most of us are far more preoccupied with this world than with the technological one. We are concerned with the relationships we make much more than with the precise mechanism by which Concorde is enabled to fly at supersonic speeds. When we read the tragic poets of Ancient Greece the emotions and the relationships they describe are as fresh and real today as they were in Periclean Athens or much, much earlier still. *This* world, which is not changing all that much, offers great scope for anyone, young or old in years, who has sufficient inner resources. Those who are young today need to continue to develop these inner resources throughout their lives. We must not commit the crime of indoctrinating the young with the view that the only expanding phase in a person's life is from infancy until a career is established, when a plateau is reached, to be followed by an inevitable downhill slide into hidebound, unreceptive, unteachable and incapable dotage.

If we are to teach the young that there are no natural restrictions, in terms of age, to a human being's development, then we should strive to provide them with example as well as with precept. We can always point to various elderly people in all walks of life who are as fully alive as anyone – but these people are considered to be remarkable in our culture and in our social circumstances. Given the opportunity to realise more of their potential, such fully alive people could – and should – become much more numerous and much less remarkable. It would become normal for people to be fully alive all their life.

At a recent conference on the role of the retired and the elderly in society, the question of continuing education was discussed, and several points were made which it may be worthwhile to elaborate a little here. Education was felt to be a somewhat awe-inspiring term, since many older people may have memories of teaching methods which were in their young days often very formal and rather harsh. There seemed to be a problem of how to set about convincing them that modern methods of education are far livelier, far less rigid and far more attractive, than they might think. With our facilities for communication through the various media I see no difficulty in projecting some factual information on how exciting and attractive learning may be in our day. The difficulty, to my mind, lies more in persuading enough people that it is worthwhile making the effort on behalf of those older people who may have doubts on the subject, and initiating the dissemination of positive information.

Another point of view expressed at this conference was that older people should not be forced into further education, because many of them were very happy to be doing nothing more than watching television or playing bingo. Certainly nobody should be *forced* into anything – but people should be *offered* a choice. If they are happy to watch television, because nothing else appeals to them as much – fine. But if they are doing this simply because they do not know what else they could possibly be doing – then it is not good enough. At a day centre in London where a great variety of activities is available, including the study of French, music appreciation, sculpting, photography and so on, the television room, in fact, became more and more deserted. In an experiment carried out in Australia to test the unfortunate theory that older people cannot learn new things, a group of retired people were given the opportunity to study German. Not only did they accept the challenge enthusiastically, and succeed in attaining university entrance standards, but this endeavour transformed their morale, their view of themselves.

The vital need for opportunities of continuing education is being recognised by those who are concerned for the well-being of older people. The best ways of providing such opportunities are being discussed. There is no doubt in my mind that eventually the best way will be to admit students, irrespective of age, to all sorts of courses and educational establishments. Educational segregation of retired people is not the ideal answer. Daytime courses are suitable for members of the freelancing population, be they retired from full-time employment, or married women wishing to acquire new knowledge or qualifications, or school-leavers taking up tertiary education. In this context, much could be done by some imaginative individual or community exchange arrangements, the commodity exchanged being *time*. Once we break out of the rigidities of thinking conventionally about education, we shall see that more can be achieved and enjoyed than we ever imagined.

A question of priorities

We are exhorted from all sides to get our priorities right whenever we want to progress in some direction or to avoid some disaster. This is sound advice. Thousands of words could be written about *how* the quality of life should be made better for older people, and many thousands more about how, say, to expand specific aspects of work opportunities, or how to provide better housing. Such details will certainly need to be worked out – but they are not top priority in themselves.

The top priority, in my view, is to establish a climate of opinion among individuals, and in society as a whole, that older people are *people* and not a separate species. The next priority would be to educate individuals and society to understand that, as with all people, older people thrive on being useful, busy and needed – and if these requirements are satisfied, then their health, strength and capacity to contribute will be retained and enhanced. The third priority would be to educate individuals and society about 'doing their sums' in a global way: to establish very carefully how the costs of one course of action may be offset by savings in another direction, to consider the costs of alternatives. These are the three priorities of principle.

Turning to priorities of practical measures, my suggestion would be that the top priority here is to establish clear and simple channels of communication and information between the older people themselves and people who are in positions which enable them to make decisions and to allocate funds. This need to have access to the top is very real, if unnecessary obstacles and delays are to be avoided. For instance, a woman who could get no satisfaction about faulty merchandise was astonished when a retired businessman at the local Citizens' Advice Bureau, whom she consulted about her problem, picked up the telephone and asked to speak to the managing director of the firm she had been dealing with unsuccessfully for weeks. Within minutes her complaint was sorted out. It needed a man who was used to going directly to the top to achieve this. Bureaucracy thrives on the timid of this earth who have not the courage or the habit to approach senior people.

Every community should have a centre for information,

consultation, advice and help where older people could go with their queries, ideas and schemes. Perhaps the Citizens' Advice Bureaux could be extended to cover this function, or separate centres could be established. The important thing is that such centres, staffed by competent, intelligent and imaginative people, who could well be recruited from the freelancing, retired population, should be under a single roof. These centres should have access to other establishments, which deal with health, housing, education, employment, and to trade unions, voluntary bodies, travel agents, and local authorities.

One often hears delighted surprise at how marvellously some club, or some activity centre, is managed and run 'by the old people themselves'. And why not? The fact that these people have reached the age of sixty or sixty-five does not mean that they have lost all their skills, gifts and administrative abilities. Older people will perfectly well provide all sorts of things for themselves, if it is recognised that they are able to do so, and a framework for their needs is established. Centres such as I referred to could call upon experts of all kinds among the retired to contribute their wisdom and their expertise to furthering the activities of the centres. There are thousands of highly qualified people in retirement: lawyers, accountants, economists, organisers, administrators, civil servants, scientists, technologists, engineers, doctors, teachers, craftsmen, artists, trade union people, who could all devote some of their time and abilities to such a community undertaking, on a paid or a voluntary basis according to their wishes or their circumstances. The quality of life of the older people could indeed be transformed by such efforts. Instead of an army (and what an army: over nine million persons!) marching, or rather shuffling, towards the endless rows of geriatric beds, older people could become a force injecting new vigour and new spirit into the life of the country. They could give encouragement and inspiration to the young, for they would be seen as a vivid example of life's continuing goodness in calendar old age. They could indeed become a part of the freelancing population, instead of adding to an ever-growing human scrap-heap. All this can happen, it will have to happen – for if it does not, then the life of the whole population will, in time, be stultified. Not only humane principles, but common sense and self-interest all point in the same direction – so there are grounds for hope.

Index

For Product Safety Concerns and Information please contact our EU
representative GPSR@taylorandfrancis.com
Taylor & Francis Verlag GmbH, Kaufingerstraße 24, 80331 München, Germany

www.ingramcontent.com/pod-product-compliance
Lightning Source LLC
Chambersburg PA
CBHW050523280326
41932CB00014B/2435

* 9 7 8 1 0 3 2 6 9 6 2 5 6 *